HAUNTED
KIRKCALDY

HAUNTED
KIRKCALDY

Gregor Stewart

The
History
Press

First published 2014

The History Press
The Mill, Brimscombe Port
Stroud, Gloucestershire, GL5 2QG
www.thehistorypress.co.uk

British Library Cataloguing in Publication Data.
A catalogue record for this book is available from the British Library.

ISBN 978 0 7509 5457 0

Typesetting and origination by The History Press
Printed in Great Britain

CONTENTS

ABOUT THE
AUTHOR

BEFORE I share the ghost stories from Kirkcaldy and the surrounding area, it is probably appropriate to give a little information about myself. I was raised in the 1970s in the town of St Andrews in Fife, a town many believe is amongst the most haunted locations in Scotland – a country that itself is considered to be one of the most haunted in the world, and so, from a young age, I have been surrounded by tales of ghosts and mysterious places. My grandfather, who was a painter by trade, initially fired my interest in the supernatural. His gold-leaf expertise led him to work on some of the most prestigious buildings in the area, such as the historic buildings of St Andrews University, the oldest university in Scotland and third oldest in the UK, and nearby Falkland Palace, the former country retreat of the Stuart monarchs, where he was involved with the restoration of the king's bedroom and the chapel. While carrying out work in buildings such as these, he used to hear some of the ghostly tales connected with them and would pass them on to me.

When the time came for me to be considered old enough by my parents to get a weekly comic (which was quite a normal thing in the 1970s and '80s), rather than choosing one of the traditional comics such as *Beano* or *Dandy*, I opted for a new magazine that was about to be released by Orbis Publishing, which was entitled *The Unexplained: Mysteries of Time, Space and Mind*. While my friends were making their weekly trips to the local newsagent to collect the latest edition of tales of mischief from the likes of Dennis the Menace and Minnie the Minx, I was eager to get my hands on the next copy of what many considered to be my 'weird magazine', so that I could read the next instalment of the stories of ghosts, monsters and myths. *The Unexplained* was published from 1980 until 1983, with over 150 magazines that combined to make a series of encyclopaedias – I have read them from cover to cover and I still own and refer to them today.

As I grew, so did my interest, particularly in the reports of haunted locations, and I started to purchase as many books on ghost stories from around the world as I could. I also took every opportunity to visit old houses and castles to hear the tales and experience the atmosphere of these buildings myself, which is something I continued to do into adulthood and, some forty years later, I still do today. Over the years, this has allowed me to build up a fairly extensive library of ghost and history books with publication dates ranging from the 1800s to the present day. I also have a collection of hundreds of photographs from the many locations I have visited.

My interest in old buildings extends beyond reputedly haunted locations; I admire them for their history and architecture as well, and so, while I frequently visit locations that I know have ghostly tales attached to them, I also visit places where I am neither aware of nor looking for any associated stories of the paranormal – I am simply looking at the building to explore and appreciate its historic significance. Even so, I am rarely without a camera and a digital voice recorder. I always take a lot of photographs and, every now and again, something I can't quite explain shows up in the photos or I am told a story of local folklore or personal experience by those who look after the properties, prompting an unplanned investigation.

I don't consider myself to have any real psychic abilities, but I do believe I have a high level of intuition. I can generally read people quite easily and often get a gut feeling when something is going to happen, and it then does. This carries across to when I'm visiting a place and I just get a feeling that something is not as it appears to be. That said, I still remain an open-minded sceptic. I am frequently asked the question 'Do you believe in ghosts?' and my answer is always the same, 'No'. This frequently surprises people who I have previously spoken to passionately about haunted locations but, until such time as I experience something that will prove to me without a doubt that ghosts exist, I cannot state that I believe in them. For the same reasons, however, I equally cannot say that I disbelieve in the existence of ghosts! My attitude is never to jump to conclusions and to keep an open mind.

During my years of visiting these historic locations I have taken numerous photographs which reveal unusual lights, I have recorded disembodied voices replying to questions I have asked during investigations, witnessed the sound of footsteps from empty rooms and corridors, heard the slam of heavy doors being closed with considerable force in a building where no doors remain and I have had personal information relayed to me via a Ouija board session but, just because I cannot explain any of these incidents, it doesn't mean I will conclude that it was ghosts that were causing them. They are, and remain, simply unexplained experiences.

My hope is to one day find out what does cause incidents such as these as I do believe there is something out there, something we do not fully understand, but I do not know what … not yet! An anonymous historian who has been quoted in several early publications tells us that 'truth is in folklore, you'll not find lies carried down the years', and that is a statement that I fully believe in. It fascinates me that these stories have been passed down from generation to generation and that they still survive today, to be passed on to future generations. In addition, the sheer number of people who claim to have encountered similar things in similar locations over the years seems, to me, to add to the validity. I do also, however, believe that as the stories have been passed on they have no doubt been embellished to increase their dramatic effect or to suit slightly different circumstances and so I feel it is important to look back to try to find the origins of the story wherever possible. In researching the stories for this book this is something that I have tried to do and, where there is no or limited written documentation, I have attempted to speak directly to those who are today connected with the buildings or locations.

Through this work, I have discovered a significant lack of documentation for many of the stories connected to the Kirkcaldy area and this has created the biggest challenge in compiling this book. A wider search for sources was required and this resulted in some of the information coming from the most unlikely sources. The last place I expected to find one of the earliest references to a haunting was in a book exploring the history of sword dancing! But there it was, just a few sentences that could have easily been overlooked, and the mention of the ghost was not expanded on at all in the book. It was, however, enough to start to piece together the original version of one of the stories of a haunting I was researching and it allowed me to see how it has changed over the centuries to become far more theatrical. This and many other stories are covered in the following pages and I do hope you enjoy them. The pictures have all come from my personal collection of photographs and postcards and, where quotes have been taken from other publications, I have stated the source so that the reader can check the originals if they wish to do so.

In addition to this title, I have written two series of books. The first being *The Haunted Explorer* series which, starting with the book *Scotland's Hidden Hauntings*, covers many haunted locations throughout Scotland. My fictional *Witch Hunter* series, starting with *Rise of the Witch*, tells the story of a powerful witch from the past being reborn in today's world and the battle the authorities have to bring her campaign of terror and destruction to an end in a society that no longer believes in magic.

ACKNOWLEDGEMENTS

IT would be nearly impossible to write a book of this nature without a lot of assistance from other people and resources, and I would like to personally thank the following for their help.

To Fife Council, who proved to be an invaluable source of information, with their libraries in Kirkcaldy and Cupar providing great resources for the research, as well as their archaeologist, Douglas Spiers, who was able to provide historical data.

To Mr and Mrs Bell of the Kingswood Hotel near Kinghorn, for their help in piecing together the details of the grey lady that haunts the hotel and the roadside outside. Their verification of the reports of haunting and personal input was of great assistance and I wish you all the best with the hotel and restaurant.

To Leonard Low, author and historian specialising in the darker side of history. It was various discussions with Leonard that inspired me to finally focus my attention on writing about the paranormal. His advice on where to locate information, along with a number of leads he provided, have, without a doubt, assisted in bringing this book together.

To Cheryl: no amount of reading books, articles and accounts of hauntings can be a substitute for real-life experiences. Thank you for sharing your story and I wish you continued happiness and peace.

To the Kirkcaldy Old Kirk Trust, who provided invaluable information relating to the Old Kirk's past.

To Ryan from Haunted Scotland, who was good enough to allow me to use evidence his organisation has obtained during their investigations. This allowed me to bring some of the stories up to date with information recently gained to add to the older accounts. I hope to work with you again in the future.

And, of course, thank you to my family. To my parents for never discouraging my interest in the supernatural and to my wife and children for their continuous support, even when I'm dragging them around old ruined castles in the rain!

And to all of the other friends and family members who offered their help and encouragement, thank you all.

INTRODUCTION

SOME SAY THE DEIL'S DEAD
Some say the deil's dead,
The deil's dead, the deil's dead,
Some say the deil's dead,
And buried in Kirkcaldy.

Some say he's risen again,
Risen again, risen again,
Some say he's risen again,
And danced the Highland Laddie.

A Jacobite rhyme

WITH the above Jacobean poem (published in the book *Popular Rhymes, Fireside Tales and Amusements of Scotland* by William and Robert Chambers (1842)) citing that the Devil is dead and lies in Kirkcaldy, it would be fair to assume that the town has a long and dark past, which would inevitably lead to numerous reports of hauntings. However, while the town certainly does have a long past, it rarely features in tales of ghostly goings-on. That is not to say there are no haunted locations: you just have to dig a bit deeper to find them.

The town of Kirkcaldy, which sits on the east coast of Scotland in the county of Fife, approximately 20 miles south from the more famous town of St Andrews and 11 miles north of Edinburgh (which sits on the opposite side of the Firth of Forth), dates back to the eleventh century when the lands were gifted by King Malcolm III of Scotland to the monks of Dunfermline Abbey. The area was rich in coal, so it did not take long for the monks to establish a settlement and, by the mid-thirteenth century, a parish church had been constructed. The coal mining caused Kirkcaldy to start growing as a community, and this was accelerated by the establishment of a harbour in a natural cove that provided shelter for ships and boats from the harsh North Sea. By the sixteenth century, up to 100 ships were based in the port, making it one of the major import and export centres in Scotland.

Rather than expand inland, the town grew along the coast, slowly incorporating smaller communities such as Dysart, Pathhead and Linktown. It is likely the town grew in this way for a number of reasons. Unlike most towns in Scotland at the time, Kirkcaldy was not surrounded by a protective wall, which meant there were no restrictions on the development of the town. The sea offered protection from attack to one side of the town and also offered the potential to develop the salt pans for the production of salt which, along with the ports of Kirkcaldy and Dysart, offered the main source of income and would have meant workers were keen to live along the coast rather than inland.

Kirkcaldy also became a major producer of linen and, in the nineteenth century, linoleum began to be produced as a floor cloth. The popularity of linoleum soon grew worldwide and Kirkcaldy was ideally placed to take advantage of this with the jute mills at nearby Dundee and an already established port that was exporting goods as far away as the Mediterranean. A local textile manufacturer, Michael Nairn, saw the potential in linoleum, but was

unable to start production straight away as the method to manufacture it had been protected under a patent. Unperturbed, and knowing that the patent only offered protection for a fixed number of years, he expanded his business considerably in 1847, constructing a large, new factory to produce painted floor cloths that was designed to be ready to produce linoleum as soon as the patent expired in the late nineteenth century. Kirkcaldy soon established itself as the main centre worldwide for the production of linoleum with Nairn's being the largest single producer.

While the production of linoleum brought employment and wealth to the town, it also brought something else which many people still associate with Kirkcaldy: a stench! It is said that, at the height of production, the unpleasant smell that was produced during the process could be smelled for miles around. This aspect of Kirkcaldy is also incorporated into poetry, with 'The Boy in the Train' by M.C. Smith telling the tale of a young boy who, increasingly excited about a trip to visit his grandmother in Kirkcaldy, anxiously asks when they will arrive. It finishes with the following lines:

I'll soon be ringin' ma Gran'ma's bell,
She'll cry, 'Come ben, my laddie',
For I ken mysel' by the queer-like smell
That the next stop's Kirkcaddy!

Unfortunately, the popularity of linoleum started to decline in the mid-twentieth century and, as a result of the reduced demand, along with the increasing prices of raw materials, most of the factories closed and have since been demolished.

A linoleum factory.

Landscape of Kirkcaldy

The main economy of Kirkcaldy is now based on the service industry and the town has in more recent years expanded considerably, inland this time, to become the largest town in Fife.

Being sandwiched between St Andrews and Edinburgh, both of which have an abundance of documented tales of the supernatural, it would be reasonable to expect Kirkcaldy and the surrounding area to also have its fair share of stories and locations. An Internet search, or a search through bookstores and libraries, however, soon reveals a total lack of written information and it would seem that the ghost stories for this area have not been previously compiled. While that made the research for this book challenging, I also saw it as an excellent opportunity to bring the stories together and to start to make some connections between them, possibly for the first time. I have provided details of the sources for the information used wherever possible, however, some of the stories have been passed down through word of mouth from generation to generation with no written accounts, and I considered them too good to miss out.

Gregor Stewart, 2014

1

RAVENSCRAIG CASTLE

RAVENSCRAIG Castle is with-out a doubt the hidden gem of Kirkcaldy. Positioned in an elevated position just a short distance from Kirkcaldy's town centre, many people pass it without even noticing due to a relatively modern development of flatted dwellings that was constructed between the castle and the road, blocking Ravenscraig from view from road users. As a result the castle does not achieve the same number of visitors that other local historic buildings attract, and visitors to Kirkcaldy miss out on the impressive site and architectural importance of the castle. Although now ruinous, it is the

Postcard showing Ravenscraig Park.

The approach to Ravenscraig Castle.

most complete castle with open public access in Kirkcaldy and the surrounding area. The castle is accessed via a path from Ravenscraig Park and, as soon as the twin keep towers joined by a curtain wall first come into view, it is easy to see how formidable the castle's defences once were. The design of these defences is very significant and gives an insight into the passion the original owner had for heavy artillery, a passion that would ironically lead to him never seeing the completed castle.

The castle was constructed for King James II of Scotland (1437–60) from plans he had prepared himself. The king was well respected as an expert in artillery and his desire was to construct a castle capable of withstanding any attack from the latest heavy guns of the time.

The rocky outcrop was chosen as the site for the castle as it offered natural protection on three sides by 100ft-tall sea cliffs. The side facing the land, deemed most susceptible to attack, was heavily fortified with walls standing some 14–15ft thick and large 'D'-shaped towers designed to deflect cannonballs. This castle would be the first in Britain that was capable of withstanding artillery fire.

King James played an active role in the siege of Roxburgh Castle in the Scottish Borders, one of the few strongholds still held by the English following the Wars of Independence. Keen to utilise his knowledge of artillery, the king had brought a number of his own cannon to aid in the battle and, on 3 August 1460, just a few months after work started on the construction of Ravenscraig Castle,

Ruin of the tower. Note the thickness of the wall and 'D'-shaped design.

one of his cannon (known as 'The Lion') exploded while being fired, causing him extensive leg injuries. Despite efforts to save him, the blood loss was too heavy and the king died a short while later. The tragedy was recorded by the Scottish chronicler Robert Lindsay of Pitscottie in his book *The History of Scotland: From 21st February 1436 to March 1565,* and states that the king 'did stand near hand the gunners, when the artillery was discharged, his thigh bone was dung [or broken] in two with a piece of misfired gun, that brake in shooting; by which he was stricken to the ground and died hastily'.

Following his death, the king's widow, Mary of Guelders, was determined to see his vision for Ravenscraig Castle completed as a tribute to him and so she continued to fund the construction while she lived in the west tower, known as the Queen's Tower. When she died

in December 1463, however, the castle remained incomplete and ownership was passed to their son, King James III, who did not seem to share the same desire to see his father's work finished. In 1470, James III passed ownership of the still-incomplete castle, along with all of its lands, to William Sinclair in exchange for the rights to the earldom of the Orkney Islands.

The Sinclair family continued the construction work at the castle, and eventually it was completed, although not entirely to the king's original design. The castle remained in the ownership of the Sinclair family and played an important role in protecting merchant ships in the Firth of Forth against pirate attacks, which were common at that time due to the Forth being home of the main docks for importing and exporting goods between Scotland and Europe.

In the 1650s, the castle suffered considerable damage at the hands of Oliver Cromwell's army as they marched north to try to take the Highlands of Scotland. After this it seems the castle was never restored and instead became a source of stones to build the cottages and houses that now stand nearby. In the late nineteenth century, the linoleum magnate Sir Michael Nairn bought the castle and its grounds and opened the entire site up as a park for the local community before gifting it to Kirkcaldy in 1929. The castle is currently owned by Historic Scotland and is open during daylight hours. Due to the low visitor numbers, the castle is not staffed and so there is very limited access within the castle building due to safety concerns.

For many years, local legend has it that a lady dressed in a long, flowing white dress has been seen wandering silently through the grounds of the castle. Given the history of the castle, this was believed for a long time to be the spirit of Mary of Guelders, still walking within the home that meant so much to both her husband and herself in life. However, an incident in the early 1980s in a hospital that sat on the ground next to the castle brought this belief into question.

The cottage hospital was built on the estate beside the castle, also by Michael Nairn, for the people of Kirkcaldy. Opened in November 1890, initially the hospital offered only ten beds, but it was later extended in 1895 and again in 1914

Ravenscraig Castle from the shore.

Inside Ravenscraig Castle courtyard.

Postcard of Cottage Hospital.

to create more bed space. The extensions were built in a circular manner, possibly to reflect the D-shaped towers of Ravenscraig, which gave the hospital a unique appearance. The ever-growing population continued to put pressure on the facilities and with no more land to extend the hospital, a new hospital was built elsewhere in the town and the Cottage Hospital was eventually closed and fell into a state of disrepair.

Shortly before its demolition in 1984, it is reported that a group of children were exploring the derelict building when they saw a lady, wearing a long white dress, gliding along one of the long corridors. The children fled but when they told people what they had witnessed, the similarity to the figure that had been seen in the castle grounds was noted. It is unlikely that the spirit of Mary of Guelders would walk the corridors of the hospital, a building that was constructed over 400 years after her death, and so the possible identity of this figure was once again questioned. It is known that both long-term patients and visitors to the hospital used to enjoy visiting the castle and its grounds, as they offered a peaceful place where they could relax and enjoy the fresh sea air. Is it possible then that the lady is actually a spirit attached to the hospital rather than the castle, who roams both the hospital building and also the castle, the place she escaped to for solitude?

Local paranormal research groups have carried out a number of investigations at the castle and have produced some interesting electronic voice phenomena results, indicating that there may be two spirits present in the castle. Their recordings include a male-sounding voice, telling them in no uncertain terms to leave, and also a female voice, that seems to be calling out for help, and this could be the spirit that is still witnessed wandering within the grounds.

2

HAUNTED HOSPITALS

THE OLD Kirkcaldy Memorial Hospital is not the only one in the area to have tales of strange happenings. In the countryside, approximately 1.5 miles to the north of Kirkcaldy, sits an unusual cluster of buildings, comprising of a large, two-storey stone-built Victorian villa and a number of newer, single-storey brick buildings to the rear. In recent years,

Remains of the Victorian Villa at Kirkcaldy Infectious Disease Hospital.

The hospital ward buildings.

these buildings, all in a very poor state of repair, have attracted a lot of attention from paranormal groups who have been keen to investigate them after persistent rumours that they are haunted.

Information on the buildings is limited but, according to Historic Scotland, the Victorian building, originally known as Crosbie House, was constructed in the mid-nineteenth century and then enlarged towards the end of the same century. It was converted into a hospital in 1902, known as Kirkcaldy District Infectious Diseases Hospital, and the single-storey buildings behind it were added over the following decade to create additional wards and facilities, including a morgue. The original Victorian building was also converted before being used as accommodation for the staff that worked there.

It is not clear exactly when the hospital closed, although town records show that a proposal to construct a new Kirkcaldy Burgh Infectious Diseases Hospital was approved in 1927, and so the closure of the existing hospital would have been soon after the new one was completed. The site was later used as a school for disabled children and then a home for boys in need of care, before the original Victorian building was converted into a hotel, with the hospital ward buildings being used for storage. From some of the documentation found lying around in the property, it also appears the building was used as a care home for the elderly at some time between the boys' home closing and the building being converted into a hotel.

The hotel building has stood empty for a number of years, with the valuation roll indicating it was vacated prior to 2006. A fire a few years later has left this once-grand building in a state of partial collapse. The hospital buildings to the rear also appear to have been left to fall into a serious state of disrepair since they were closed.

I was able to visit the buildings several years ago and so, despite the lack of early documentation relating to any supposed hauntings, I built up a good picture of the location. The whole site has quite a sinister feeling, with numerous children's toys lying around both inside and outside the buildings. To add to the eerie feeling, these toys include many headless dolls with the heads found elsewhere on the site, so it would be easy to allow your imagination to run wild. It seems the teams of investigators focus on the hospital buildings to the rear rather than the Victorian villa, and a number report feeling as though they are being watched, unexplained noises and the figures of both a man and a woman seen in different parts of the complex.

Having visited, it is clear to me why the site has gained a reputation for being haunted. The hospital is known to have treated a number of unpleasant conditions, such as typhoid, which can cause considerable pain and particularly horrendous deaths. The property, therefore, has a suitably distressing past for a traditionally haunted location. The condition of the buildings and the children's toys throughout also add considerably to the atmosphere. However, when taking all things into account, I remain unconvinced that this is a truly haunted location.

The buildings were used for a number of purposes after the hospital closed yet, despite this, there seems to be no record of any reports of strange occurrences prior to the closure of the hotel and the site being abandoned. It was not until later,

The ward buildings – derelict and spooky.

Inside a ward at Kirkcaldy Infectious Disease Hospital.

when the property became a magnet for local youths looking for somewhere to go at night, that the claims of ghosts began to build momentum and the paranormal investigation teams started to take an interest. I do wonder whether the initial reports of strange goings-on were actually different groups of youths trying to scare one another on this large site. That said, I remain completely open-minded regarding this location. It could be that reports grew because people were once again visiting the buildings after dark and experiencing genuine occurrences.

I have included details of the hospital in this book as, despite my own reservations, many people do believe it to be haunted and so I will continue to monitor new information that comes from this location in the hope that more conclusive evidence can be provided or that earlier records are found providing reports of earlier experiences while the buildings were in use.

I must add that the buildings on this site are in an extremely poor state of repair and under no circumstances should anyone enter the site. It is fenced off to prevent entry and there is a genuine danger of real harm throughout. The buildings can be viewed from the roadside, but please respect the privacy of those who live nearby.

3

THE CASTLES AND CAVES OF WEMYSS

THIS cluster of three small villages sharing the name of Wemyss are situated a few miles north east of Kirkcaldy. Despite their small size, they boast an impressive number of historically significant locations. The villages – West Wemyss, Coaltown of Wemyss and East Wemyss – all grew as mining communities,

Remnants of a coal mine outside Kirkcaldy.

Entrance to the Dovecot Cave.

initially with salt mining and later coal mining. The mines were owned and operated by the Wemyss family, who had established the clan seat in the local area.

The name Wemyss is believed to be derived from the old Gaelic word for caves and was selected due to the oldest of the historically significant sites, a series of twelve prehistoric caves with many containing wall carvings dating back to the time of the Picts. As well as being used for shelter, these caves have had numerous uses including as a dovecote, storage, a spa, a court and a glass factory. The importance of the caves was recognised in 1937, when they were given the status of a Scheduled Ancient Monument under the Ancient Monuments Act 1931. More recently, in 2004, they were the subject of an episode of the Channel 4 archaeological programme, *Time Team*. There are two

stories of hauntings related to the caves, but, as they are more directly connected to other locations in the villages, it is appropriate to explore these places before relaying the ghost stories.

As well as the caves, the Parish of Wemyss boasts three castles. One is situated in the gardens of the current Wemyss Castle and unfortunately has no recorded stories of hauntings related to it. Wemyss Castle itself sits on the coast between West and East Wemyss and Macduff's Castle sits to the north of the region. Wemyss Castle is the most impressive of them all, with the oldest part of the castle dating back to 1421, when it was built on behalf of Sir John Wemyss. Over the centuries the castle has remained the seat of the Wemyss clan, with the castle being considerably altered and extended to form the impressive stately manor house that stands today. There have been many occasions on which royalty have visited the castle, the most famous of which was probably Mary, Queen of Scots' visit in 1565 when she first met her future husband, Lord Darnley. Today the castle remains a private family home and is not open to the public; the grounds, however, are open at certain times and allow visitors to view the restored gardens. It was during a school visit to the castle and gardens in the late 1970s that I first heard the story of the ghost of Wemyss Castle, which would make it one of the earliest stories I heard and one that helped spark my interest in the paranormal.

The castle ghost is probably one of the best known in the local area, described as a tall, young woman wearing a long, flowing, green dress, known as Green Jean. Little has been discovered regarding who Green Jean may have been in life or in what way she is connected to the castle. When I first heard the story of Green Jean I was told that she appeared as a warning that the head of the clan was nearing death, yet further research indicates that this is not necessarily the case with several reported sightings not connected to the death of the clan chief. There are, however, reports that the Wemyss family do have a warning of death in the form of masonry falling from the walls of Wemyss Castle, and it is possible these two tales have become intertwined over the centuries. Green lady spirits are sometimes considered to protect families (which would make it strange to suggest the appearance of Green Jean to be a sign that the clan head is nearing the end of his life), but this can also be considered as a warning so any family affairs can be put in order, securing the future of the clan.

Wemyss Castle from the shore.

Postcard showing Wemyss Castle.

One of the Wemyss caves, which lies below the castle, is known as Green Jean's cave. The entrance to the cave has, however, been sealed up and sightings of the spirit are mainly reported within the castle itself. Unusually for a ghost, many people describe a feeling of calm along with an inability to speak while in her presence, which is frequently announced by the sound of her dress 'swishing' as she glides.

A reported sighting of Green Jean is noted in the autobiography *My Memories and Miscellanies* by the Countess of Munster, Wilhelmina FitzClarence (née Kennedy-Erskine), published in 1904. Wilhelmina, born 1830, was the third child of the Honourable John Kennedy-Erskine and Lady Augusta FitzClarence, an illegitimate daughter of the Duke of Clarence (who later became King William IV). In 1855 she married William George FitzClarence, the second Earl of Munster. This was

a double wedding with her sister, Millicent, marrying James Hay Erskine Wemyss on the same day, and it was through her sister that the encounter with Green Jean was relayed.

The Countess of Munster recalls the story of the sighting told to her by her sister that took place while a large party of guests were staying at Wemyss Castle over the Christmas period. Keen to ensure her guests were kept entertained, Millicent had set up a stage in the large dining room to provide some theatrics and had travelled to Kirkcaldy to collect some props, leaving her daughter and a friend at the castle. When she returned, the two girls ran to meet her, shouting that they had seen Green Jean.

They told her they had been sitting chatting beside the fire in the dining room when they heard a rustling noise. They both looked towards the stage, where the noise had come from, and watched as the curtains parted and a tall, pale-looking lady wearing a green dress walked out onto the stage. They reported that the lady held a lit Egyptian lamp in front of her and, ignoring the presence of the two girls, made her way across the stage to a door at the side, before opening the door, walking through to the next room and closing the door behind her. Throughout, the only sound that could be heard was the swishing of her long dress. The girls had sat silently watching but, once the door was closed, had become quite excited as they knew the room the lady had entered was a store used by the butler and that there

was no other way out. They rushed over to the door with a lit candle to illuminate the room, but when they checked, they found it to be completely empty.

Millicent feared the encounter with Green Jean would cause some concern among her guests and so she ensured the story was kept quiet; however, she was soon to witness the ghost herself. She told the countess that, on the night in question, the weather had been stormy. Her son had been out riding all day and, as he had been feeling unwell earlier, she had stayed up late to make sure he returned safely. After hearing

Sealed entrance to Green Jean's Cave.

him enter the castle and make his way to his private sitting room and then on to his bedroom, both of which were situated next door to Millicent's own private sitting room, she waited for around half an hour. When all was quiet, she went through to check on him and, satisfied that he was sound asleep and well, she proceeded to the long gallery to return to her own quarters.

Her attention was drawn to some movement and she saw a tall lady dressed in green walking silently towards her with just the sound of her dress moving. She did not recognise the lady as one of the guests staying at the castle and the thought crossed her mind that it must be Green Jean. Feeling calm, she waited until the figure reached her and she then walked along the gallery beside her, intending to take the opportunity to question the ghost. Green Jean is said to have turned her head away from Millicent as they walked and, despite her wish to ask questions, she found herself unable to speak. At the end of the gallery, Millicent found herself alone again, with no sign of Green Jean and the gallery completely empty. She recalled feeling frustrated at being unable to speak, but took some comfort from the fact she had at least been able to walk with the ghost, something she doubted many people would have been able to do.

Further reported sightings of Green Jean are included in *County Folklore*, volume 7 (1912), which provided details from an article written by the Duke of Argyll titled 'Real Ghost Stories' for the *London Magazine*, published in November 1901. The encounters are said to have been described to him by the late Miss W (Wemyss?) who lived at the castle. Miss W, he tells us, was 17 years old when she had her first encounter with the phantom. She had been sitting chatting with a joiner who was carrying out some work in a small room, accessed from the billiard room. It was late in the evening and the joiner was working by the light of a lamp, alone. When Miss W left and returned to the billiard room, where the only source of light was the fire burning in the fireplace, she was struck with a feeling of being watched. She looked around and, at the opposite end of the room, saw a misty figure. As she stood and watched in silence, the figure walked towards her and she noted that, as it passed the fire, there was no change in the appearance of the figure, as though the light of the fire had not illuminated her in any way.

The lady continued to walk towards her until she was about 10ft away, before turning and walking through the wall. The same figure was seen twice more in the same week, once in the passage upstairs (possibly the same gallery where Millicent had her encounter with the ghost) and later in another room in the castle, although no further details are given of either of these encounters. Despite these tales referring to the figure as the 'Green Lady', curiously the detail within indicates she appeared in grey rather than green and there is no mention of the 'swishing' sound that had become associated with Green Jean. This would lead me to suggest that the ghost encountered in these instances may not have been Green Jean after all, but instead one of the other ghosts believed to haunt the castle.

In her autobiography, the Countess of Munster also recalls a story told to her by her sister-in-law that took place many years before Millicent had her encounter with Green Jean. She was told that while her sister Millicent was heavily pregnant, her husband, James, suffered ill health. Millicent's pregnancy was a difficult one and she had gone to bed early to rest, leaving her husband and his sister talking, planning a trip to London. As they spoke, they were said to be looking out of the window (which overlooked some new terraces being built in front of the castle) at the view across the Firth of Forth. James had just commented that he was starting to feel particularly unwell when they heard a crash and saw that part of the terrace had collapsed, to which James - recalling that falling masonry predicted the approaching death of the owner of Wemyss Castle - said, 'I am a dead man.' Although his sister dismissed the incident, James died two weeks before Millicent gave birth to their youngest son.

A few miles from Wemyss Castle, on the outskirts of the village of East Wemyss, lie the ruins of Macduff's Castle. The original castle on the site was built in the eleventh century for the powerful Macduff family, the Earls of Fife, a family perhaps better known today for their connection with Shakespeare's play *Macbeth*, which is based on accounts that Macbeth killed King Duncan of Scotland in 1040, after which he became the King of Scotland.

Macduff is said to have been unhappy with the situation and went to England, where Duncan's wife had fled with their young children, to help prepare her young son, Malcolm, to return to Scotland and retake the crown. When he returned to Scotland, accompanied by an army to help Malcolm take the throne, Macduff discovered that Macbeth had murdered his wife, Lady Macduff,

Postcard showing Macduff's Castle.

Remains of Macduff's Castle.

and several of their children. Macduff pursued Macbeth and eventually caught and defeated him in 1057, avenging the murder of his wife and children and allowing Malcolm to take his rightful place as king. While there are many reports that the slaying of Lady Macduff and her children took place at Macduff's Castle, records indicate the castle was not built until after King Malcolm took the crown and so the slaying must have happened elsewhere.

The Wemyss family mentioned earlier evolved from the Macduffs and the castle and its lands passed into the ownership of the Earl of Wemyss. The oldest part of the castle that still stands is the west tower, which was home to Sir Michael Wemyss and was visited by King Edward I of England, who stayed there in 1304.

With the first War of Independence not yet settled, after King Robert the Bruce started his battle to restore the Bruce family to the Scottish throne, Sir Michael changed his allegiance from the king to support Bruce's campaign. King Edward was said to have been enraged by this act and ordered his army to destroy the castle. Ownership of the extensively damaged castle passed to the Livingstone family and, over the coming centuries, the castle was restored and extended. The castle then passed to the Colville family during its restoration and remodelling until, in 1637, it was bought back by the Wemyss family.

As they had already established nearby Wemyss Castle as their family home, Macduff's Castle was not used as a principal residence. With a general lack of maintenance, the castle started to deteriorate and this was allowed to continue until it was ruinous. In 1967, the army were called in by Fife Council to pull down one of the towers due to it being considered dangerous. The sole tower that still stands is also now in a dangerous condition and, although it can still be accessed, great care must be taken when visiting.

The castle is believed to be haunted by a grey or white lady, thought to be the spirit of a young servant named Mary Sibbald. According to the legend, Mary was the daughter of a wealthy family from the west of Fife but fell in love with a member of a band of Gypsies that passed through the area. She was so smitten that she ran away with the Gypsies and married her lover. The Gypsies set up home in one of the Wemyss caves, as was a common occurrence in those days, and Mary managed to get work as a maid in the castle above. When some fruit went missing, Mary was accused and her trial took place in the Court Cave, overseen by the Baron Baillie. Mary was found guilty of the theft and she was sentenced to receive twelve lashes of the whip.

The punishment was carried out immediately and Mary – a fragile young lady who, before running off with the Gypsies, had enjoyed a privileged upbringing – was never to recover from her injuries. She was taken to the Well Caves, which sit directly below Macduff's Castle and take their name from a natural well believed to have healing waters, but with a mixture of infection in her wounds and shame at what had become of her, Mary died in the caves.

The caves beneath Macduff's Castle.

Inside the Court Cave, where Mary Sibbald's trial was held. Note the brick pillar recently added to support the cave.

In a popular version of the story, as told in several books (including *Of Kindred Celtic Origins* (2001) by J.K. Scales), among those who witnessed the first sighting of Mary's ghost was King James V, who is widely believed to have frequently disguised himself and travelled throughout Scotland to experience life as a 'common man'. It was on one of these outings that the king met a band of Gypsies in the Wemyss caves. He took the opportunity to join them to see how they lived and, before long, the drink began to flow. There were suspicions within the group that Mary had not stolen anything, and that the real thief was still among them but had chosen to stay quiet and allow Mary to take the blame and the punishment. With the alcohol starting to take its toll, the finger of blame was pointed at a woman named Jean Lindsay, who was the former lover of Mary's husband. She denied it and a heated argument broke out that only stopped when a lady dressed entirely in white appeared within the cave, at which point the Gypsies fled the cave and Jean confessed to the crime.

King James was said to have immediately gone to the castle above and, after revealing his true identity, informed the Baron Baillie of what he had just witnessed in the cave. As he described the lady in white and her soft, blue eyes, the baron froze and then explained that he too had been haunted by the vision of those same eyes since the day of the trial.

Even after Jean Lindsay confessed as the true culprit, reports continued to be made of sightings of Mary Sibbald's

Jonathan's Cave, the area where the skeletons were found.

ghost, always dressed in either white or grey, being seen both within the castle and in the cave. Several rather more recent accounts say she has been seen staring out of a window in the upper level of the west tower. With no floors or stairs remaining in that tower, it would have been physically impossible for anyone to be there. After this tower was demolished by the army, there have been no further documented sightings of the ghost.

There are several claims that Mary's body was buried within one of the Wemyss caves, which may explain why her ghost continued to be seen long after she was proven to be innocent. With this in mind, I have made enquiries with the Archaeology Department at Fife Council and they have confirmed that three skeletons were found at the Wemyss caves. The most recent two were found in the 1980s and in the 1990s, both close to a cave known as Jonathan's Cave. These skeletons have been carbon dated and both were shown to be from the twelfth century and so cannot be connected to the story of Mary Sibbald. The first skeleton, found back in the 1850s, is perhaps more significant to the story. It too was found close to Jonathan's Cave, which is a short distance from the Well Caves where Mary died. This skeleton was described as being 'a relatively recent burial', due to the condition of the bones and the presence of some hair.

What 'relatively recent' means in archaeological terms is open to interpretation. The connection with James V would place these events as occurring some time in the first half of the sixteenth century, which may well still be classed as 'relatively recent' archaeologically. There is little information as to the condition of the skeleton or the amount of hair found but it is well documented that, in certain circumstances, hair can remain on a skeleton for hundreds of years indicating that, just maybe, this skeleton could be connected to the story of Mary Sibbald.

Although the ghost has not been sighted for some time, in 2013 a paranormal investigation group visited the castle and carried out some trials of a new communication system. They received several responses to questions they asked, including a female voice saying 'I'm back'. Perhaps sightings of the ghost will soon begin anew!

4

HAUNTED HOMES

IT would seem that Kirkcaldy has more than its fair share of ghostly encounters reported from private homes. A lot of the claims include footsteps being heard, interference with electrical items and items being moved and, while in many of these reports the full address of the property is not stated to ensure the privacy of the homeowners, some addresses, or at least the streets, are known.

One such report, as published by Haunted Scotland, relates to a series of incidents that occurred in an upper flat in Leslie Street, a normal street in the Linktown area on the southern edge of Kirkcaldy. There is nothing unusual about the buildings in Leslie Street; they comprise mainly of four-in-a-block flatted homes, built by the local authority as social housing around the 1950s, in a style used throughout Kirkcaldy and, no doubt, Scotland as a whole. The occurrences reported by the occupants in one of the properties were, however, extraordinary.

The tenant began to notice instances when he was sitting watching television and the volume would suddenly start to increase, despite no one being close to the television set. Although no date is given, local enquiries would indicate these incidents occurred some time ago, most likely prior to the time when remote controls started to become a standard feature with television sets and when you still had to get up and physically press a button or turn a dial to adjust the volume. This would rule out the possibility of someone accidentally leaning on the remote control or a faulty unit and it no doubt caused a considerable nuisance for both the tenants of the flat and the occupants of the property below. The tenants also started to have problems with the lights, which would turn on and off on their own. As the property was owned by the local authority, these incidents would have been reported to them as the landlord, but the contractors seem to have been unable to find a fault in order to resolve matters.

Things were to take a more sinister turn for the tenants, however, when a large, shadowy figure began to appear. It is described as being approximately

6ft tall and most often seen moving from the bathroom to one of the bedrooms. At the time the tenant's father was staying with them and was sleeping in the bedroom in question. The figure seemed to most commonly appear when he went to bed for the night, leading to the belief that it was in fact following him and on one occasion it was seen standing at the foot of his bed. The witness described it as having a smoky consistency, but fled before they could see whether it would manifest to have more visible features.

There is no obvious explanation as to what might have caused the property to be haunted or who the figure may be. It is not a historic building (the upper floor is actually relatively newly built) and there is no indication the site has any past history that would result in the land being haunted. Haunted Scotland report only one further incident, when the child of a later tenant of the property was said to have been scratched while sleeping in the bedroom. No details of the severity of the scratch are given and,

without further details, it is not possible to rule out the child scratching themselves in their sleep. Considering the information available, particularly the comments regarding the shadowy figure, I would suggest that any reports of hauntings at the property are more likely to be connected to the father rather than the building.

A similar conclusion can be reached concerning the report of a ghostly encounter in another haunted house in Kirkcaldy. Again, this took place in a flat within the Linktown area of the town. This time it was Buchanan Court, an estate which is estimated to have been built in the 1960s (making it a more recent development than Leslie Street) and consists of blocks containing multiple flats. Although there were previously buildings on the site, there is nothing in their history that would explain the encounter a couple had with what they referred to as 'the Strangling Monk of Buchanan Court' in the online magazine, *The Kirkcaldy Book*.

Leslie Street.

Buchanan Court.

Although others claimed to have seen a hooded figure in the property, the focus seemed to have been on the woman of the house, who frequently claimed to wake up gasping for breath. She described the feeling of someone climbing on top of her as she slept and feeling pressure around her throat, as though cold hands were pressing hard, at which point she awoke. This continued to happen for some time until, on one occasion, her husband woke to the sound of his wife gasping. When he looked over to check on her, he is said to have witnessed her face being pressed into the pillow and 'something on her back'. He screamed in terror and whatever was there vanished. He does not seem to have ever offered any description of what he saw and whether that is from fear or if, as been suggested, it was erased from his mind, will never be known. After that occasion, no further sightings of the hooded figure or incidents of attacks on the occupants were reported at the property.

It would be easy to suggest that the wife was encountering sleep paralysis, a natural and not uncommon phenomenon where people awake to find themselves temporarily paralysed and unable to move. This can last for anything from a few seconds to several minutes and, during the time when it is believed the body is in a state between sleep and being awake, sufferers often have a sense of dread and even hallucinations that an intruder is in the room. These hallucinations can frequently be reported as demon-like and, in the past, sleep paralysis was believed to be visitation by demons rather than a natural occurrence. The result is frequently panic and anxiety, including shortness of breath, which may explain the wife's belief that she was being strangled. I have experienced this myself and know how frightening and real it can seem. However, in this particular case, other witnesses also claim to have seen the hooded figure in the property and sleep paralysis cannot explain her husband's experience.

Whatever it was they were experiencing, after the husband witnessed it, there was never any recurrence.

A further report of a haunted house comes from a street named Oak Tree Square. Like Leslie Street, the properties in Oak Tree Square were built by the local authority, initially as social housing, although many have since been purchased and are privately owned. The homes in this area are semi-detached and terraced houses rather than flats. Researching old maps of the area, the properties seem to be built on former farmland, and so there is no indication of anything untoward in the area. Fortunately, on this occasion, the experiences of the occupants were recorded both in the *Journal for the Society for Psychical Research,* Volume 40, and by the local press, which provide more accurate reference points.

The incidents started in February 1958 and lasted until September of the same year although it is unclear what triggered them or why they stopped so suddenly. It is, however, noted that the family had a girl who was 12 years old at the time, leading to this being compared to classic poltergeist activity. I am sure anyone reading this book will have heard of a poltergeist, but not everyone may know what one actually is. There is no disputing that documented encounters recorded as poltergeist activity are unpleasant and frightening for all of those involved, or that poltergeists are considered to be a malicious form of spirit; however, they are not generally the evil, demonic spirit depicted in Hollywood blockbusters.

What does differentiate a poltergeist from a standard haunting is the level of activity involved. Common signs

General shot of Oak Tree Square.

of a poltergeist include unexplained but purposeful noises such as bangs on hard surfaces, objects moving around the property, unexplained electrical disturbances (including items switching on even if they don't work or are unplugged), strange smells and, only in the most extreme cases, some physical attacks such as scratching or pushing. The term poltergeist is derived from two German words, *poltern*, which means to make noise, and *geist*, which means ghost, and so, quite literally it means a 'noisy ghost'. Most reports of poltergeist activity seem to revolve around children who are either approaching or are in their early teenage years, particularly girls.

Initially the disturbances at Oak Tree Square were limited to the sounds of footsteps from parts of the house where there was no one present. Bangs and thuds were also heard throughout the house, again from areas where there was no one there to make the noises. This went on intermittently for some time and then seemed to escalate, with drawers in the house being found to have been opened and, on some occasions, windows in the property opening apparently on their own. During the night of 11 September, the presence made a final show of strength by moving a chair and a wardrobe in one of the bedrooms. Although no one witnessed this, the report by the Society for Psychical Research notes that the householder checked the property at around 2.30 a.m., at which point everything was in order, yet the following morning the furniture had been moved.

The society do raise the question of whether the 12-year-old girl, who first reported the displaced items, may have moved them herself, but they conclude that, if she had been physically responsible for the escalation of the incident, it would seem unusual for her to have waited for around six months before deciding to do so. It should also be noted that no one in the house heard the furniture move and that a wardrobe from the 1950s, or older, would not have been easy for a 12 year old to move at all, let alone silently.

It would seem that after this event, the family were left in peace and what had caused the disturbances remained unknown. An interesting observation was, however, made by the *Journal for the Society for Psychical Research* who revealed that, on the same morning as the furniture was moved in the property at Oak Tree Square, poltergeist activity started around 20 miles away in a cottage in St Andrews. It is said that this took the form of small objects appearing to be thrown around a bedroom and this went on for two nights. Could it be that the poltergeist, having caused some disturbances in Kirkcaldy, moved on to the property in St Andrews to terrorise a new family?

The final account of haunted goings-on in a house in Kirkcaldy comes from the best possible source, the homeowner. While reading documented accounts of incidents is both useful and interesting, nothing is more informative than speaking to the people who have actually experienced what has happened first hand. The property in question is a substantial stone-built house in Victoria Road. Although it is now relatively central in Kirkcaldy, in the late nineteenth century when the property was constructed, Victoria Road was the outermost street in the town.

The family moved into the house around eighteen years ago, prior to which an elderly couple lived there for

Victoria Road.

many years before moving to a smaller property in the town. When the current owners moved in, they commenced a complete refurbishment of the property, including replacing floorboards, the kitchen, bathrooms and redecorating the bedrooms. In the kitchen there was a mezzanine level and it was while carrying out work to the stairs that the disturbances seemed to start. Initially this took the form of footsteps that were heard walking about on the mezzanine and on the stairs leading to it, often sounding as though they started about halfway up the stairs. On other occasions, while the homeowner was alone in the house relaxing, watching television or reading a book, she would hear someone whisper her name directly into her ear but when she looked around she would discover there was no one there. The family also started to notice a strong, passing smell in the house as though someone was smoking, although there was no one in the family who did. On numerous occasions, all members of the household caught a glimpse of movement out of the corner of their eyes, but when they looked directly at what they thought they saw, there was nothing there. One bedroom in the house was particularly difficult to heat, even with modern central heating, and while the homeowner's son was using this room, he suffered badly with nightmares.

One particularly interesting incident occurred in full daylight. The homeowner explained that she had just finished mopping the kitchen floor and had hung her mop outside to dry in the sun when she heard the telephone ringing. She went through to the hallway to answer the phone and, as she chatted, she noticed some movement in the kitchen. She had a clear view of the mop bucket through the open kitchen door and she watched as it started to 'wobble'. She could see there was no one near to the bucket and, with the mop removed and outside, there was nothing in it to cause any imbalance. The bucket was also still full of the dirty water from cleaning the floor, so any draughts would not be sufficient to cause the heavy bucket to move. As she watched, the bucket suddenly tipped over, spilling the water all over the floor.

They still have regular experiences with hearing footsteps, whispers and seeing glimpses of movement around the house, but the family are now relatively used to it all. They do not feel that the entity means them any real harm and so have come to accept it as part of living at that property.

It does, however, remain unanswered as to who, or what, haunts the property. There are signs that could result in it possibly being classified as a poltergeist; however, although the incident with the mop bucket does indicate a mischievous side to this case, this is the only incident of that level to have occurred. In addition, the homeowner's child was not in the typical age group associated with poltergeists when the activity started, and their children have now grown up in the house, yet the activities remain. The elderly couple that lived in the house previously have unfortunately both passed, and so it has not been possible to ask whether they experienced anything in the house.

The homeowner was, however, able to supply some information that may shed some light on these mysterious goings-on. She was told the patch of ground to the rear of the property is known as 'hangman's gate' and was the location for Kirkcaldy's gallows. I have searched a number of old maps but have been unable to find any reference to this area being marked as 'hangman's gate', although this type of title is more commonly a local reference to a specific area rather than a formal name. I have found several references to people being hanged at 'the gallows above the town' and this would certainly tie in with the gallows being in the elevated position of Victoria Road which, even on a map dated 1855, is shown as being outside of the town boundary. A site outside the town could well have been chosen in the hope this would prevent the spirits of the condemned from re-entering the town. Incidentally, while the map from 1855 does not indicate a gallows, it does show a slaughterhouse on the site. Perhaps this location was chosen as the ground had already witnessed killings.

Whatever the cause of the disturbances in the property, the important thing is that the occupants do not feel threatened by it and do not feel uncomfortable in the house they so lovingly restored. I am extremely grateful to them for taking the time to talk to me.

Stories of haunted houses are not limited to Kirkcaldy itself; the surrounding area also has several reported cases. Haunted Scotland gives an account of strange happenings in a ground-floor flat in Dysart, a town which is now considered a suburb of Kirkcaldy, in the 1990s. Normand Road, Dysart has a wide range of properties along its length ranging from larger detached homes to flats. Most are older buildings of stone construction, formerly used as housing for the coal mine workers and their families. As seems to be a common theme, the disturbances at the property in Normand Road started with a series of fairly minor incidents that could easily be dismissed as

Normand Road.

natural occurrences. One such example was the tenant returning home from work to find the television was on, but he would just put this down to forgetting to turn it off before he left in the morning. In addition to these incidents, it was said the tenant had a constant feeling that he was not alone in the property, and someone was watching him.

After staying at the property for several months, the tenant had a particularly frightening experience. Initially it seemed like one of the other incidents in the house, when he awoke one morning to find his bedside light switched off. That may not seem at all unusual, except he was certain he had left it on the night before, but still he dismissed it as probably just being a blown bulb. To check, he tried to switch the light back on and, to his surprise, it was working, so someone must have switched

it off during the night. No doubt feeling unsettled about the light, he got up and went through to the living room to find it in a state of total disarray. The television set was turned so it was side on from its normal position, all the ornaments in the room had been moved with several placed on top of the television set and most of the furniture had also been moved, with the cat litter being placed beneath a stool. Fearing he had been broken into, he checked all of the windows and the door but found that everything was still locked, with no damage, and that he was alone in the house. He sat in the armchair while trying to rationalise what had happened and, at this point, his cat caught his attention. It was staring at him and then seemed to look up and over his shoulder, arch its back and start to hiss. At that point, he fled the property.

Fearful about what was happening in the flat, the tenant called in a psychic medium who, after walking around the house, told him that an elderly former occupant had not moved on and remained in the property. The psychic claimed that it was the spirit of an old man who was trying to make contact with the tenant, which was why he had been turning on the television and moving things around. That seemed to have been enough, however, for the tenant, and he moved out a short time after.

According to Haunted Scotland, neighbours claimed that later tenants also left the property rather quickly, although this cannot be independently confirmed to have any connection to ghostly goings-on. With no recent reports it would seem that whatever was causing the disruption has settled down again. As for the tenant who experienced this unexplained activity, Haunted Scotland reports that, shortly after moving into the flat, he had started to go through a particularly unhappy time in his life. This seems to match the time when the unusual incidents began to become more frequent and so may have been the trigger, with the tenant admitting that such negative energy might well have fed whatever caused the disruptions.

The tales of haunted homes are not restricted to more recent years; there are several accounts in historical books. One such example is *County Folklore*, Volume 7 (1912) and relates, in detail, to the old manse of Kinglassie, which lay about 2 miles to the west of Kirkcaldy. Unfortunately the building has now been demolished and so it is not possible to explore it further, but reports from the time refer to an entity known as the 'Kinglassie Devil'. The most common occurrence was said to have been a sudden, extremely loud noise from one of the upstairs rooms described as sounding as though a 'cart of stones had been tipped onto the floor'. No explanation was ever found for this noise and it seems it was being caused specifically to distress those in the house, indicating poltergeist activity. One particular incident occurred on a cold night, when the minister had held a meeting of the church elders in the manse. One member had, on arrival, complained about how cold it was outside and had taken off his boots to warm his feet at the fire when the noise from upstairs was unleashed. He was so terrified that he jumped from his seat and badly burned his feet in the fire.

There is also said to have been a haunted house that stood on the banks of Loch Gelly, around 3 miles west of Kirkcaldy. Rather than being haunted by a former resident, the spook that walked the grounds of this property was that of a magnificent white horse. Many people made a connection that the horse may be a kelpie, a spirit from traditional Scottish mythology that appears in the form of a horse on the banks of rivers and lochs, encouraging those who see it to climb onto its back. As soon as they do, the kelpie gallops into the water to drown and devour its victim.

There are no tales that I can find that would give an indication as to why a horse would haunt the grounds, although it is always possible that a previous resident owned a horse that died in sudden or tragic circumstances, the sort of situation that not only results in reports of human hauntings, but for animals also. The horse is not the only animal said to have haunted the grounds of the house;

Loch Gelly, site of the animal hauntings.

one resident was said to have been so taken by the appearance of the phantom horse that, on her death bed, she vowed to return to also remain in the garden, yet for some reason said she would return as a mole. The belief that she had returned seems to have influenced future residents, as they are reported to have avoided interfering with the moles in the garden and to have allowed them to dig freely.

A particularly sinister haunted house tale comes from Burntisland. The story was told in the *Weekly Scotsman* magazine in 1896 and reads as follows:

I lately heard a weird story that may interest many of the readers of the Weekly Club. My grandmother actually saw all the events related here, and told them to me a few weeks before her death. The only conditions she imposed on me were that I should not make known the story publicly until after her decease which she felt was fast approaching, and that if ever I did so, I should not publish any name in connection with it. Being now released from the first condition, I relate the story as it was told to me, with but few revisions, hoping that if any reader can throw any light on the matter or add fresh facts, he will oblige by letting us know. Here, then, is the story:

Shortly after I married, my husband and I went to live in an old spacious house opposite Burntisland, about half a mile from the coast. The day on which these wonderful events happened was a wild December one. My husband had gone to Dunfermline on business, and the servants were all out, for one reason or other. So I was left alone for the first time in that great house. After an extra furious gust of wind, I was roused by a noise at the door. On opening it I was startled to see four unknown men, dressed like seamen, march in without a word, carrying the apparently lifeless body of a young lad. They carried him upstairs into a small bedroom at the back of the house. They halted beside a large cupboard that occupied one side of the room, and, while two men held the boy, the other two moved a small camp-bed that was near beside the cupboard, and laid the boy gently thereon. Then all four marched out.

All this time I was watching, dumb with astonishment. Not a word had been spoken by them through the whole proceeding, and the few words I spoke were received in silence. A few minutes after the men left, a young lady, apparently about twenty-five, with a beautiful and expressive face, ran into the room. She was dressed in an antiquated style of dress of rich and elaborate material. I can yet remember every detail of the scene, so vividly was it impressed on my memory, although that was more than fifty years ago.

I was roused by the sound of the girl speaking violently to the lad, who had just recovered from his faint or whatever it was, and I stepped forward to ask an explanation, when, to my horror, I saw the boy's face through the body of the girl. It was with an effort that I kept myself from fainting, but managed to seat myself in a corner of the room and await developments.

'Jack, Jack!' I heard her say. 'He is coming. Hide yourself. He is within a hundred yards of the house.'

'I cannot, Agnes,' he said, with a look of terror and fatigue. 'I am too weak, and there is nowhere to hide.'

'Hide in here,' she said, rapidly opening the door of the cupboard, and, pressing a spring at the back, revealed a dark opening. 'Quick now, my poor boy,' she said, tenderly, helping the boy in at the same time.

She had just time to close the spring door and the door of the cupboard when the door of the room was opened violently, and a tall, stern-looking, black-bearded man strode in. 'Where is the boy?' he shouted. Receiving no answer, he took a small dagger from his belt and repeated his question. This time the girl firmly refused to give any information, so without a moment's hesitation, he plunged the dagger into her heart. Instantly all vanished, but before I could recover myself I heard a scratching proceeding from the cupboard and agonising cries of despair. I tried to rise and go to the cupboard, but in vain; my limbs refused to bear me. I fell back, and remembered no more until I awoke with my husband standing over me. When I was able I told him the whole story, and together we searched the cupboard. After much searching, we found the spring, and on opening the spring door discovered a few mouldering bones and a large but illegible manuscript.

J.E. Harris, Weekly Scotsman, *26 December 1896*

According to the magazine, these sightings were treated as a dream, until the caretaker for the property also witnessed the same incident being played out in front of his eyes, at which point it was decided to demolish the house and the site was levelled and planted with wheat crops. Without details of the location of the house, it has not been possible to investigate these events further. This, however, is a classic example of a residual haunting, where events of the past were so traumatic that the negative energy they created are believed to have been 'imprinted' in the atmosphere of the place and are replayed like a recording. Although most residual haunting involve only sounds, the physical appearance of those involved can occur, but in such cases there will be no contact between those re-enacting the past events and those witnessing the re-enactment. In this story, the murder of the girl and subsequent starvation of the boy would certainly appear to be tragic enough to have resulted in the energy of those involved to remain, which is believed to be what causes a residual haunting.

For the final haunted house story, we return to Kirkcaldy itself. This story was reported in the book *The Night Side of Nature: or Ghosts and Ghost Seers* (1904) by Catherine Crowe:

A very remarkable circumstance occurred some years ago at Kirkcaldy, when a person, for whose truth and respectability I can vouch, was living in the family of a Colonel M. at that place. The house they inhabited was at one extremity of the town, and stood in a sort of paddock. One evening, when Colonel M. had dined out, and there was nobody at home but Mrs M., her son (a boy about twelve years old), and Ann, the maid (my informant), Mrs M. called the latter, and directed her attention to a soldier who was walking backwards and forwards in the drying-ground behind the house, where some linen was hanging on the lines. She said she wondered what he could be doing there, and bade Ann fetch in the linen, lest he should purloin any of it. The girl, fearing he might be some ill-disposed person, hesitated; Mrs M., however, promising to watch from the window that nothing happened to her, she went; but still apprehensive of the man's intentions, she turned her back towards him, and hastily pulling down the linen, she carried it into the house; he continuing his walk the while, as before, taking no notice of her whatever.

Before long the Colonel returned, and Mrs. M. lost no time in taking him to the window to look at the man, saying she could not conceive what he could mean by walking backwards and forward there all that time? Whereupon Ann added, jestingly, 'I think it's a ghost, for my part!'

Colonel M. said, 'he would soon see to that,' and calling a large dog that was lying in the room, and accompanied by the little boy, who begged to be permitted to go also, he stepped out and approached the stranger; when, to his surprise the dog, which was an animal of high courage, instantly flew back, and sprung through the glass door, which the Colonel had closed behind him, shivering the panes all around. The Colonel, meantime, advanced and challenged the man repeatedly, without obtaining any answer or notice whatever; till at length, getting irritated, he raised a weapon with which he had armed himself, telling him he 'must speak, or take the consequences,' when just as he was preparing to strike, there was nobody there! The soldier disappeared, and the child sunk senseless to the ground.

Colonel M. lifted the boy in his arms, and as he brought him into the house, he said to the girl, 'You are right, Ann. It was a ghost!' He was exceedingly impressed with this circumstance, and much regretted his own behaviour, and also the having taken the child with him, which he thought had probably prevented some communication that was intended. In order to repair, if possible, these errors, he went out every night, and walked on that spot for some time, in hopes the apparition would return. At length he said that he had seen and had conversed with it, but the details of the conversation he would never communicate to any human being, not even to his wife. The effect of this occurrence on his own character was perceptible to everybody that knew him. He became grave and thoughtful, and appeared like one who had passed through some strange experience.

The above named Ann H, from whom I have the account, is now a middle-aged woman. When the circumstance occurred she was about twenty years of age. She belongs to a highly respectable family, and is, and always has been, a person of unimpeachable character and veracity.

This initially would have appeared to have been a residual haunting, as the figure of the soldier seemed to have been unaware of the presence of the maid when she went out to bring in the washing and he had no interaction with her. After the intervention of Colonel M., however, it would appear the haunting was actually intelligent, and the spirit of the soldier was able to interact with him. The tale is printed as a sign of the power of the will, showing that the colonel's perseverance to try to communicate with the spirit resulted in the eventual discussions that are claimed to have taken place. Whether it is possible to convert a residual haunting to an intelligent haunting through persistent intervention is not documented, although from this tale it would appear to be feasible if one is determined enough.

Please remember that the properties covered in this section are all private homes. In order to maintain the privacy of the owners and occupiers, the photographs shown throughout are general shots of the streets involved and are provided solely as a visual aid for the reader to illustrate the general appearance of the area. They do not show the specific properties.

5

THE TOWN CENTRE, PUBS AND HOTELS

KIRKCALDY'S industrial past resulted in several public houses becoming established close to the factories and mills to allow the workers of the day to enjoy well-deserved refreshment and the opportunity to relax after a hard day of physical labour. Some of these pubs still remain today, and with such a long history it is not surprising to hear that there are reports of strange and unexplained occurrences happening within

Betty Nicols public house.

at least a couple of the buildings, indicating that some of these former locals may not yet have given up on their regular visit to the pub.

One of these premises lies towards the north end of Kirkcaldy high street, where you will find the Betty Nicols public house. The building has been occupied by and operated as a pub since at least 1741 when it was known as the Victoria Bar and, during the centuries that it has been trading, it has changed hands several times between the main brewers until, in 2002, it was sold and is now privately owned.

The pub retains many of its original features which creates a pleasant 'olde worlde' atmosphere. It does, however, seem that the building has kept more than just its charm, with numerous unexplained occurrences being experienced by both the staff and the customers. The incidents were reported in the *Fife Free Press*, and the article is quoted on the pub's website as follows:

Whisky and vodka aren't the only spirits that can be found at Betty Nicols this year. For the Kirkcaldy pub has its very own ghost according to members of staff, who have witnessed some spooky goings-on. The pub, located on the east end of the High Street, has been in existence since the early 18th century and is no stranger to ghostly incidents.

But just before Christmas, cleaner Vikki Drysdale got the fright of her life when she arrived for work a little earlier than usual. When she entered the back room as part of her daily routine she jumped out of her skin when she saw a tea light burning on one of the tables. CCTV footage also showed a flame flickering when previous images from throughout the night had shown nothing.

Vikki said: 'I came in early, about 7 a.m., and went through to check the back room. When I opened the door it was pitch black but I noticed that one of the candles was burning. I got a fright and panicked – there's no way a tea light that size could have burned all night. I blew it out and quickly shut the door. I definitely think there is a ghost here. Every time I go into the back now I'm a bit edgy. I have never been back through that early since, and the barmaids don't like going down to the cellar for ice anymore.'

The article goes on to describe the experiences of one of the barmaids who work at the pub. She was able to confirm the general dislike of the cellar area among the staff and their reasons for this with Jo Dalton, barmaid at the pub, saying: 'I've not had a direct experience with the ghost but you certainly get a feeling of a presence down in the cellar as if someone is watching you.'

One of the other barmaids does, however, appear to have had a direct encounter with the spirits in the bar (as well as the ones on the shelves!). She claimed to have seen the ghosts and the article continues to describe her experience, and some of the other occurrences, as told by the bar's owner, Sandy Haxton:

Our other barmaid Vicky maintains there is definitely a psychic presence in the pub. She claims that she can see the ghostly figures of two men and a dog walking about. We've had other members of staff hearing bells and seeing figures in the mirror. I'm not really into any of this rubbish but after looking at the tape I'm beginning to believe it myself! It's bad enough trying to get staff just now without freaking them out with ghost stories.

With seemingly regular reports such as these, it is not surprising that the bar attracted the attention of paranormal organisations, some of whom have been given the opportunity to carry out investigations in the premises, during which they have reported hearing unexplained noises, along with experiencing dropping temperatures in the cellar with no apparent cause. The *Fife Free Press* reported one visit by the respected psychic caseworker, Archibald Lawrie, to the premises:

> Archibald Lawrie, author of the *Psychic Investigators Casebook*, visited Betty Nicols last June with a medium to give a talk on his new book. He said that they detected spiritual movements during their visit. 'I'm called to various sites to get rid of spooky things. I chat to the spirits and they tell their story before moving on, and in Betty Nicols we definitely felt the presence of memories from the past.'

Whatever or whoever is causing these unexplained events remains a mystery. The figures are yet to be identified by witnesses but, with investigations ongoing, hopefully there will be some answers provided soon.

Betty Nicols is not the only haunted bar in Kirkcaldy. Just outside the town centre, in the Pathhead area, sits the Feuars Arms. Like Betty Nicols, the Feuars Arms has operated as a public bar for many years. The former flourmill was converted in 1859, with the exterior of the building being extensively rebuilt in 1890. In 1902, the interior of the property was remodelled in an art deco style with decorative tiles, including two inset figurative panels by Doulton, a mosaic flooring, stained-glass windows depicting the arms of Scotland, England and Ireland and even a glass cistern and marble-framed urinals in the gents' toilet! Perhaps the most prominent feature of the pub is its 18m-long bar counter, lined with art deco tiles. These finishes remain today and were considered to be historically significant enough to have been included in the records held by Historic Scotland when the building was listed. The internal features of the building were also included in the Historic Scotland publication *Raising the Bar*, published in June 2009.

The reports of unexplained occurrences in the Feuars Arms include the sounds of items being moved around in empty areas, footsteps being heard as though someone is running down the stairs towards the kitchen area but, when checked, it is found no one is there, beer pumps turning themselves off and the sound of a woman singing. In February 2005, a local paranormal group carried out an investigation at the pub, accompanied by a reporter from the *Fife Free Press*. The landlord at the time advised that, in addition to the experiences already listed, there had also been incidents where staff felt as though someone touched them on their shoulder when there was no one else present. It was also claimed that one particular section of the cellar always felt cold, no matter how warm the rest of the cellar or building was. On one occasion the landlord took his dog down into the basement and, as they approached that area, the dog was said to have become distressed and 'freaked out'.

The investigation team who attended the property reported seeing a number of light anomalies during the night, as well as hearing some tapping noises and one

Feuars Arms public house.

member stated that she felt someone touch her on the shoulder, but when she looked, there was no one near her. However, according to the article in the newspaper, the most interesting occurrence took place when they carried out an experiment with a glass, which was placed upturned on top of one of the tables in the bar area. The team repeatedly called out to any ghosts in the building and requested that they demonstrated they were present by moving the glass and, after a short time, it is said the glass did slide a few inches across the table. No one was touching the glass at the time and the table had not been moved or inadvertently knocked. This incident

was witnessed by all those present and, to date, no natural explanation has been found for the glass apparently moving on its own. With seemingly high levels of unexplained phenomena occurring within the Feuars Arms, it continues to be of interest to the paranormal community and, hopefully, investigations will continue and eventually some answers will be provided.

Returning to Kirkcaldy town centre, a retail unit currently occupied by the British Heart Foundation is reported to have ongoing unexplained happenings. The shop is based in a grand three-storey building in one of the oldest parts of the town, on the corner of Kirk Wynd and the High Street, and is known as the Swan Memorial Building. Constructed in 1895 to commemorate Patrick Don Swan, who was the provost of Kirkcaldy for thirty years, it was later altered in 1930 to create the shop unit on the ground floor, which remains today. Unfortunately, these alterations resulted in the visual impact of the property being reduced. However, you just have to look up towards the unaltered first and second floors to see how impressive the building once was.

The reports that come from this property describe sightings of the ghost of a young girl, most commonly encountered in the basement. It is believed that she is the spirit of a child who was struck by a horse and cart outside the building. After the accident, she is said to have been taken inside the building so her injuries could be tended to, and she is most likely to have been treated in the basement, out of sight of the occupants of the ground floor, where, sadly, she died.

Attempts to gain additional information on this story have so far yielded no results and no records seem to exist of a child being killed in that area under the circumstances described. What has been documented, however, were earlier

concerns raised regarding the condition of the road outside the building, which had already resulted in the tragic death of Dr John Martin on 4 September 1837. Dr Martin had been returning from the opening of a new church in the nearby village of Milton of Balgonie, and was thrown from his carriage near the top of the brae when the horse pulling the carriage bolted. Dr Martin struck a wall and died two days later from his injuries. Ironically, at the time of his death he had been in discussions with the town council regarding carrying out improvements to Kirk Wynd which was described as only being a street as far as the church, beyond which it was nothing more than a winding footpath.

When considering the corner plot this building occupies, along with the confirmation that horse-drawn carriages did use the roads outside, regardless of their condition, and that an earlier accident using this method of transport had resulted in the death of Dr Martin, it would be easy to envisage a horse and cart thundering down the relatively steep Kirk Wynd, at the bottom of which is a tight turn into the High Street. With the unpredictable nature of horses, and the risk the driver could easily misjudge the speed at which

Swan Memorial Building with the British Heart Foundation shop on the ground floor.

they were approaching the blind corner, any street children playing in the area would have had to move fast to get out of the way of the horses. If it was a street child who had been hit, it is entirely possible no record of the incident was made. Unfortunately, without further details it has proved impossible to investigate this story further.

Further up Kirk Wynd sits the Old Kirk, the oldest building in Kirkcaldy. The earliest written records of the church are believed to be from 1244 when Bishop de Bernham, from nearby St Andrews, consecrated the building to St Patrick and St Brisse (St Bryce), although the site is known to have been used for Christian worship for many centuries before this. The oldest part of the building that still stands is the fifteenth-century tower, with the main church building being added in 1807. This is described by Historic Scotland in their listing details for the property as a 'good example of the re-use of older ecclesiastical buildings during this period', giving a clear indication that earlier buildings stood on the site, with tradition indicating the first church building here was built by St Columba in the sixth century. The graveyard around the church is also one of the oldest in the area, with gravestones dating back to 1522.

The church itself served the local community for many centuries with those attending ranging from the ordinary people of the town to well-known names of the time, such as the famous and influential Scottish political economist and philosopher Adam Smith, who was

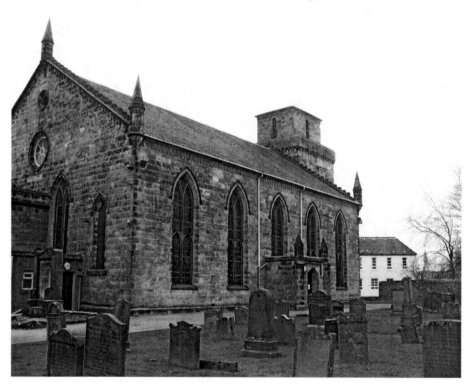

The Old Kirk.

The ancient tower at the Old Kirk.

christened in the church on 5 June 1723. Also among those who rest in the Old Kirk's cemetery are the Swan family, as mentioned in the section covering the haunting at the British Heart Foundation shop, and Michael Nairn, who started the Nairn floor covering business. In the year 2000, the Old Kirk merged with nearby St Brycedale church and in 2010 the church was closed, bringing almost 800 years of Christian worship on the site to an end. In 2011 it was sold by the Church of Scotland and was acquired by the Old Kirk Trust, which continues to preserve the building for the local community. Members of the Old Kirk Trust were also good enough to provide me with some information relating to the building, including reported ghost sightings.

The Swan family tomb.

Plaque celebrating Michael Nairn.

Contrary to many people's expectations, it is actually relatively rare for a church or a churchyard to be haunted. These are generally considered to be places of rest and peace, whereas most reports of haunting are from places where a wrongdoing was carried out or where there was a sudden, unexpected death, ranging from accidents to gruesome murders. Where a tragedy has occurred within a church, however, that can give rise to claims of hauntings within the building, and the Old Kirk is no exception.

Disaster was to strike the church during the evening of Sunday, 15 June 1828. Reverend Edward Irving, a prominent clergyman who had strong connections with Kirkcaldy, having previously set up a school in the town's Oswald's Wynd, had returned to deliver some sermons. During his time away he had become quite famous and, on his return to Kirkcaldy, a large crown of curious locals attended the church, keen to hear him preach.

The church building is said to have been filled to capacity with more people gathered outside. As Reverend Irving entered the church, the crowds in the galleries are reported to have surged forward to catch a glimpse of him. The sudden increase of weight at the front of the balconies caused the beams supporting them to pull out of their supports in the walls and a substantial section of the north gallery collapsed. This resulted in panic among the crowds, with those still on the galleries trying to get back down the stairs and out to safety, while those in the main section of the church were also trying to escape, fearful that more of the balconies could collapse. In the tragedy, the falling beams killed two people, twenty-six people were trampled to death in the escaping crowds and approximately 150 people were injured.

The ghost that has been reported from the kirk appears to be a lone figure standing in the church. This figure has been witnessed on a number of occasions, although fuller details are somewhat sparse, which would lead me to believe that most people only catch a glimpse of the ghost out of the corner of their eye rather than seeing a full-blown apparition in front of them. The figure is normally seen in the south-west corner of the kirk, indicating it is unlikely to be the spectre of one of those killed by the falling beams from the gallery. It is, however, possible that it is the spirit of one of those who were crushed to death in the resultant stampede as people attempted to escape. Another possibility worthy of consideration is it may be a mourner rather than someone killed in the church. Anyone standing in the south west would look towards the north of the church, where the balcony collapsed, and so it is possible this is the spirit of a relative of one of those killed in the tragedy, forever grieving and looking over the place where they lost their loved one.

Dunnikier House Hotel

On the northern edge of the town, surrounded by parkland, stands Dunnikier House Hotel. This Georgian mansion house was constructed between 1791 and 1793 for James Townsend Oswald, a prominent former politician. The Oswald family previously resided at a mansion in the Pathhead area, also known as Dunnikier House; however, having grown increasingly concerned at the continuing growth of Kirkcaldy towards his property, he had a new home built away from the developing part of the town. The original Dunnikier House was renamed Path House and is now operated as a medical practice for the National Health Service.

The Oswald family continued to be a dominant political force in the Kirkcaldy area throughout the nineteenth century and several members of the family also went on to become well-decorated senior officials in the military forces. In 1938, after the death of Colonel St Clair Oswald, the local authority purchased large parts of the estate as a housing site to meet the increasing demand for housing in the area. Ironically, the land was to be used for the expansion of the town, the very thing that the house was originally built to avoid. In 1944, the town council also purchased Dunnikier House, initially for use by the Ministry of Defence prior to the building becoming the base for the Parks Department. In 1971, it was converted into a hotel and it was sold to the current owners in 1994, at which time it is noted in the records compiled by Historic Scotland as having become 'very run down'. Since then, the hotel has been completely and sympathetically restored to its original condition and is once again a grand country house.

Since operating as a hotel, there have been several claims of experiences with the paranormal from both staff and guests. These include a grey lady, a common name given to female apparitions who appear mist-like, or grey, in appearance. The identity of the grey lady is not known and she is mainly reported in certain rooms within the hotel, as well as walking the passageways between them. There do not seem to be any reports of the ghost interacting with anyone who sees her, indicating that she is a residual spirit who appears to be carrying out an action she performed in life.

The same cannot be said for a number of strange occurrences in the kitchen

Path House.

area of the hotel where it is said there is a particularly active spirit that is rarely seen but is very keen to make its presence known and interact with others in the vicinity. This type of haunting is known as an intelligent haunting, where the spirit is said to be aware that others are in the area and they wish to, in some form, communicate. It could also be classed as a poltergeist, and reference has been made by some of those I have spoken to about the hotel to 'the poltergeist'. A particularly unusual incident is said to have happened during an investigation carried out by the paranormal investigation group, Scottish Paranormal: it is claimed that the utensils that hung on the wall in the kitchen started to move as they watched, in such a fashion that they were described as appearing to be 'dancing' in front of them.

Again, the identity of any ghost responsible for what it witnessed in the kitchen remains a mystery and so, in an attempt to gain further details, I spoke to former staff members, who confirmed that the most common incidents were items moving about or completely disappearing from the kitchen area. There was also an additional story provided, which relates to one of the hotel's bedrooms (although I will not state which one). Several guests who have stayed in this room report having awoken during the night to find a small girl sitting on the end of their bed. Again, there does not seem to be any interaction and the girl simply disappears, although it must be a frightening experience for those who witness her. It is possible the spirit of the child is connected in some way to that of the grey lady.

Dunnikier House Hotel.

It would seem logical to conclude that all of the ghost encounters in the hotel relate back to the Oswald family as they were the first and only occupants of the building until it was bought by the local authority with several members of the family passing within its walls. With the building continuing to be used as a hotel with regular guests staying, it is hoped that further details of these hauntings can be collected and that paranormal groups will be allowed to carry out further investigations that may shed some light on the identity of the spirits and the reason they remain.

6

BALWEARIE CASTLE

ABOUT 2 miles outside Kirkcaldy, on the edge of the golf course, is the site of the ruins of Balwearie Castle. All that remains today are a few walls of the original tower house that give no indication of the grand building, full of mystery and fear, that once stood there.

The folk song 'The Wronged Mason' provides the story behind a haunting at the site and tells of a mason who, having carried out work on the castle, was not paid and so sought terrible revenge. The original author of the song is unknown, and it has been published in many forms and quite possibly extended from its original form. According to the book *The Legendary and Romantic Ballads of Scotland*, edited by Charles McKay and published in London in 1861, the earliest known publication of 'The Wronged Mason' was in 1776 in a collection compiled by a Mr Herd from Edinburgh.

It tells of the mason Lamkin who was hired to work on Lord Wearie's castle but never paid for his troubles. After Lord Wearie travelled overseas, Lamkin teamed up with a nurse (nanny) who worked for the lord and lady who allowed him access to the castle. The lady of the house was upstairs and refused to come down but their baby son had been left unattended downstairs. To bring Lady Wearie down, Lamkin drew his knife and cut a deep wound in the baby's body, ensuring that he would cry out loudly in pain. After Lady Wearie was warned by Lamkin that the only way to stop the baby's suffering was for her to come downstairs and face him, she eventually did so and was immediately confronted by Lamkin who, encouraged by the shouts of the nurse (known in the ballad as either the false nurse or false nanny), murdered her. The baby also died from his wounds. When Lord Wearie returned from his travels some months later, he was told what had happened and he set about hunting down and capturing Lamkin and the nanny. Lamkin was hanged from the tree outside the castle and the false nurse burned at the stake.

With such an unpleasant subject matter, it is difficult to believe that the ballad was sung for entertainment and many feel that

The ruins of Balwearie Castle.

it was created as a means to strike fear into children to stop them straying from their homes in case Lamkin came after them.

The tree referred to in the 'Wronged Mason' would have been a Dule Tree. The name 'Dule' means grief or sorrow and was given to trees that were used as gallows for public hangings. Many castles and grand houses at that time had such trees within their grounds, which not only provided the physical means to carry out executions, but also created a visual reminder to all working on the

estates of the fate that they may meet, even for a minor crime, if they did not abide by the rules. Although no sign of such a tree on the site remains today, in the *Ordnance Gazetteer of Scotland: A Survey of Scottish Topography*, edited by Francis H. Groome and published in 1884, specific reference is made to a large yew tree close to Balwearie. It is quite possible that this tree was used as a Dule Tree, and certainly likely that this is the tree said to be haunted by the spirit of Lamkin, who is said to have appeared as a dark shadow forming the outline of a hanging man swinging silently from one of the branches. If this is the ghost of Lamkin, one could understand why his spirit has not moved on but remains in this realm, given the grotesque nature of his alleged crimes. With no mention of any more recent sightings, it would, however, seem that the phantom vanished when the tree was removed.

It is believed that Balwearie Castle was home to Sir Michael Scott, the Great Wizard of the North during the thirteenth century. Sir Scott's powers were said to be so great that he could summon and control both demons and spirits to use as he wished. It seems he was not content with making an already haunted castle his home as, according to the legend, he brought with him a number of ghosts over which he had acquired control during his journeys throughout Europe, and he used these ghosts to serve guests during the many banquets he held at the castle.

After his death in a freak accident, there was no further mention of these spectral servants within the castle and so it appears that, upon his death, they were released from his control to return to where they originally came from.

Near to the castle stood a rocky outcrop known as Bel Crag with a cave situated below it. This cave was predominantly avoided by superstitious locals, who believed that it intermittently blew air from both heaven and hell, described as a 'breath from heaven or a blast from hell'. It was said that if you could control your breathing enough so that you inhaled these airs in the correct quantities, they would give you the ability to see events in the future. Even travellers knew to avoid the cave or passed it with haste, as the air coming from the cave was thought to have an almost hypnotic effect on those who dwelled too close by.

The seventh volume of *County Folklore*, published in 1912 for the Folklore Society, tells the tale of the phantom piper who is said to haunt the area. The incident leading to the haunting was said to have occurred 'about a century ago', which would place it at the start of the 1800s. The story tells that a piper was returning to Kirkcaldy from a fair at nearby Lochgelly, where he had been drinking heavily. The weather was stormy but, despite this, as he passed the cave, instead of hurrying past as most people did, he paused and looked inside. The air coming from the cave seems to have had an effect on the piper as rather than continuing with his journey, he raised his bagpipes and started to play in an attempt to drown out the noise of the wind.

The harder the wind blew, the louder the piper played the pipes, which are said to have become enchanted from the air in the cave, forcing the piper to continue playing. The music was described as 'wild and unearthly' and the piper was unable to stop until sunrise the following morning, when a farm labourer was walking to work and found his body lying at the mouth of the cave. The mouthpiece of his pipes was said to still be between his lips as though he was still playing at the moment he died. Although all traces of Bel Crag have now gone due to the ground being quarried for stone, it is said that, on stormy nights, the sounds of the piper's frantic piping can still be heard being carried in the wind.

7

TESTIMONY OF THE DEAD

IN SCOTLAND, there used to be a practice where the dead were allowed to stand trial and to give evidence in court cases. One famous case of this occurred following the events on 5 August 1600, known as the Gowrie Conspiracy, during which John Ruthven, 3rd Earl of Gowrie and his brother, Alexander, are said to have lured King James VI to Gowrie House with the intention to kidnap him. The attempt was unsuccessful and, in the resultant fight, both John and Alexander Ruthven were killed. Shortly afterwards, the order was given that the brothers' bodies were to be embalmed and they were taken to Edinburgh, where they stood trial for treason. The fact the two men were already dead and could not offer any defence seems to have been irrelevant, and in due course they were both found guilty, with the punishment for treason being execution. The two corpses were then hung, drawn and quartered.

In Kirkcaldy, although not a traditional ghost story as it did not involve the appearance of a phantom, there was an event in which it appears the spirit of a dead man returned to his corpse to give evidence during a trial. The case is recorded in both the *Domestic Annals of Scotland: From the Reformation to the Revolution* by Robert Chambers, published in 1874, and the book *County Folklore*, Volume 7 (1912) and is said to have occurred on 16 June 1662.

A Kirkcaldy malt man named George Grieve, while operating the malt kiln, was shot in the head by his son. The reason for the murder is believed to have been an unfortunate conclusion to a series of arguments the father and son had been having. In an attempt to conceal the murder, the son loaded his father's body onto one of his horses and rode to a nearby bridge, where he threw the body into the river below.

Unfortunately for the son, the body was found the following morning and the officials brought him in, along with his mother, as suspects for the murder. As it was believed the dead man could assist in identifying his killer, the body was brought before them and both were asked to touch him. Nothing happened, but the belief was that the body would not identify the killer until at least twenty-four hours had passed since the death. As the authorities did not know how long the body had been in the river, the suspects were held for several more hours before again being asked to touch the dead man. As soon as the son placed his hand on the body, the corpse is said to have started to bleed from the nose. When he removed his hand, the nosebleed stopped.

The son continued to plead his innocence, maintaining he had no knowledge of the murder and so his mother was once again asked to touch the corpse. She did so, and nothing happened. Still denying any involvement, the son was once again told to place his hand on his father's body, and the nosebleed returned. The bleeding corpse was considered sufficient evidence to prove the young man's guilt and he subsequently confessed that he was the killer, and that his mother had nothing to do with it. He was sentenced to death and hanged in Kirkcaldy.

Another tale from the area relating to the recently dead originates in the village of Auchtertool, which lies approximately 3 miles west from the edge of Kirkcaldy. The church of Auchtertool sits around another mile west of the village itself, which may appear unusual, as churches often form the centre of village communities. A likely explanation for this is that the church sits on a site that had been used for religious purposes long before Christianity was introduced into Scotland. Indeed, in the history of

Auchtertool church.

Auchtertool parish church, it is specu-lated that this elevated location, with clear views across the countryside and to the Forth Estuary beyond, may have been used by early sun-worshipers. When Christianity was brought to the country, it was not unusual for places of earlier religious worship to be uti-lised by the Christian faith, which is believed to have been the case when the church at Auchtertool was established in 1178. Approximately 1 mile north of the church, surrounded by farmland, the remains of Halyards Castle can be found, a once palatial home for the various notable families who ruled the lands around and from which the ghost story originates.

The castle was once believed to have been the local residence for the Bishop of Dunkeld. By the mid-sixteenth cen-tury, it was home to the Kirkcaldy family, until in 1573 (following the execution of Sir William Kirkcaldy of Grange) it was passed to Sir John Boswell of Balmuto. The Boswell family seat was, however, at nearby Balmuto Tower, which sits just a few miles away, and so, in 1617, the castle and lands were passed to the Forbes family. It was then, through mar-riage, passed to the Skene family in 1628. In 1715 the castle was sold to the Earl of Moray, who never took up permanent residence and so the castle began to fall into a state of disrepair.

According to legend, some time after the Scottish Reformation, a body was brought from France to Halyards Castle. The deceased is said to have been a member of the Skene family and per-mission had been granted by the Earl of Moray for Halyards Castle to be used to store the body until burial. This was all carried out in secret as the inten-tion was for the burial to take place in accordance with the Roman Catholic

The remains of Halyards Castle.

rites, something that would not have been allowed by the Protestant leaders of the time. Late at night, under the cover of darkness, the body was then taken to the church. To minimise the chance of anyone in the village seeing it and potentially asking questions about what was happening, it was instead carried straight across the fields to the church in a torchlit procession. After the ceremony, the body was placed in the family crypt in the church. With there understandably being no documentation available to provide details of the burial, the identity of the deceased is not known; however, the route taken across the fields is now being referred to as the Lady's Walk which suggests that it was a female member of the family. A young Walter Scott, who later grew to become the famous author, was also said to have attended the funeral, which would place it as occurring in the late eighteenth century.

The secrecy of the funeral seems to have left its mark on the area as it is reported that, on the same night in August every year, a shrouded coffin can be seen being carried from the ruins of Halyards Castle, across the fields towards the church illuminated by the flames of torch bearers. Some versions of the story tell of the procession being accompanied by a piper, dressed in the tartan of the Skene family and playing an ancient tune. It would seem highly unlikely, however, that a piper would have ever accompanied a funeral that was being carried out in secret, and so this would seem that this was added to embellish the traditional tale. Although there are no recent reports of sightings of the unusual events from that night, in one telling of the story it is said that it would 'never do' for any of residents of the parish to doubt it takes place as recorded, and it remains a part of local lore.

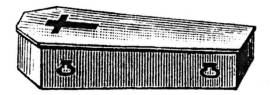

8

DEATH OF A KING

A few miles south of Kirkcaldy, sandwiched between a modern caravan holiday park and the sea, an inconspicuous stone pillar stands at the side of the road, topped with a cross and bearing a small plaque. Although most people pass it without a second glance, it does in fact mark the location of an unfortunate accident that would lead to the Wars of Independence between Scotland and England.

King Alexander III was just 8 years old when, following the death of his father, Alexander II, he was crowned in July 1249. A number of noble families in Scotland seized the chance to try to gain the position of guardian for the young king, which would allow them to influence his decisions for their own benefit, and it was not long before King Henry III of England also saw an opportunity to gain control of the Scottish crown. In 1251, when he was 10 years old, Alexander was married to King Henry's daughter, Margaret. A prolonged attempt by King Henry followed to try to persuade

his son-in-law that he should recognise the English monarch as having supreme power over the Scottish crown. However, despite his young age, Alexander resisted and he eventually took full control of the Scottish crown in 1262, when he reached the age of 21.

Alexander's first act was to continue his father's fight to regain control of the islands off the west coast of Scotland, which were held by Norway. He sent a fleet of ships to attack the Isle of Skye, which resulted in King Haakon of Norway sending a much larger fleet to regain the island in 1263. Knowing the sizeable Norwegian fleet could easily defeat his own, Alexander arranged for peace talks to take place on the Isle of Arran. All was not as it seemed, however, and rather than the talks being an attempt to settle matters, they were part of a plan to delay a battle that was almost inevitable – Alexander knew that if he could prevent any attack until the late autumn when the weather started to turn, it would reduce the effectiveness of the Norwegian fleet.

Alexander III monument.

It was a gamble that paid off and talks lasted until September before finally breaking down. The Norwegian fleet, which consisted of around 120 ships, had amassed in the Firth of Clyde and on 1 October 1263, before they could launch an attack, the first storm of winter hit the west coast. It has been described as a fast moving, powerful storm, which broke up the unprepared Norse fleet and ran many ships aground close to the town of Largs. The remaining forces attempted to salvage the damaged ships and cargo but were attacked by the waiting Scottish forces while doing so. The resultant battle, which has become known as the Battle of Largs, was inconclusive with neither side being able to claim victory.

Eventually the Norwegian ships, having been unable to get themselves into a proper battle formation, retreated to the island of Orkney off the north-east coast of Scotland, where King Haakon planned to stay for the duration of the winter and rebuild his forces before returning in spring to attack once again. However it was not to be, and the king fell ill, dying in December 1263. This was to be the last Viking attack on Scotland as Haakon's son and heir, Magnus, had no desire to retake the western isles and three years later he withdrew any claim on them in return for a sizeable payment and control over Orkney and Shetland.

Alexander and Margaret went on to have three children: two boys and a girl. In 1275, however, Margaret died and, by 1281, both sons had also died. Their daughter, also called Margaret, had married King Eric II of Norway, the eldest son of King Magnus, and in 1283 further tragedy was to strike

when she also died while giving birth to their daughter, who was also named Margaret. This left Alexander with no direct heirs and, in 1285, determined to have a male heir, he married Yolande de Dreux, the daughter of a powerful French family.

The following year, on 19 March 1286, Alexander had been attending a meeting in Edinburgh while Yolande was staying at Kinghorn Castle. By the time the meeting finished, it was dark and stormy and Alexander was advised to stay overnight at Edinburgh. The following day was Yolande's birthday and, choosing to ignore all advice, the king set off on his horse to ride back to Kinghorn to be with Yolande. The route took him along a cliff-top road and, shortly before he reached Kinghorn, it seems his horse either stumbled or was frightened, possibly by the weather, and he was thrown from the horse and over the cliff edge. His body was found the next day at the foot of the cliff. Yolande was pregnant at the time, but she miscarried the child shortly after the death of her husband and so the situation remained that there was no direct heir to the Scottish crown.

This plunged the country into a state of chaos with rival nobles, including Robert Bruce (grandfather of King Robert the Bruce), claiming the right to the throne. Norway also claimed that Alexander's 8-year-old granddaughter, Margaret, the Maid of Norway, was the rightful heir. Eventually, Norway turned to King Edward of England for assistance in finding a solution and he ruled that Margaret should return to Scotland and marry his son. Realising this could result in the kingdoms of England and Scotland being united, the Scottish nobles instead agreed to accept Margaret alone as the rightful heir with the marriage deferred and a ship was duly sent to Norway to collect her and bring her back to Scotland. During the journey back from Norway, Margaret fell ill. She was taken to the Orkney Islands but she never recovered and died on 26 September 1290, leaving no obvious heir to the throne and resulting in the many bloody battles for power that followed.

The monument to commemorate the importance of King Alexander III's actions to regain the western isles and the end of a period of prosperity and the years of bloodshed that followed his death was erected in 1886. It also marks the approximate area where his body was found.

There are two ghosts closely associated with the death of Alexander III. The first is said to have appeared at his wedding to Yolande at Jedburgh Abbey in 1285 when it is said that a phantom appeared at the celebrations that followed the wedding ceremony. Descriptions of this ghost vary; in the *Scotichronicon*, written by Walter Bower in the 1440s and sourced from the *Scottish Highland Dance History – Encyclopaedia II*, it is described as follows:

> Bringing up the rear was a figure regarding whom it was difficult to decide whether it was a man or an apparition. It seemed to glide like a ghost rather than walk on feet. When it looked as if he was disappearing from everyone's sight, the whole frenzied procession halted, the song died away, the music faded, and the dancing contingent froze suddenly and unexpectedly.

Over the following centuries, the tale of the incident at the wedding changed from the above, somewhat understated, early account of the ghost to a dancing skeleton which terrified the women and unnerved the gentlemen before progressing on to the belief that the figure was in fact one of the guests who had taken the masquerade ball costume a step too far and had chosen to turn up dressed as a skeleton, such as described in the 1838 *Gazeteer of Scotland* by Robert Chalmers which reads:

> In the year 1285, Jedburgh was the scene of the festivities which attended the second marriage of Alexander III; when a masker, resembling the usual skeleton figure of death, joined in one of the dances, and had such a powerful effect upon the nerves of the queen, and the rest of the revellers, as to cause the ball to be suddenly closed.

(Library of Congress)

73

Despite the differences in the descriptions of the spectral figure, what is consistent is that it was said to have danced at the wedding, leading to the belief that this is one of the earliest recordings of a 'dance of the dead', which is said to be a warning that one is approaching death. Although the description of the incident in the *Gazeteer* may be seen as an attempt to dispel the suggestion that the figure was anything supernatural, the author does go on to cover the suggestion that it was a death omen and says:

> Though afterwards ascertained to be a mere jest, this strange apparition made a deep impression upon the popular mind, and was afterwards held to have been an omen of the childless bed of Alexander, his early death, and the consequent mishaps which befell his country.

The choice of words, to initially state it was a jest and then refer to the figure as an 'apparition', is interesting. It is also highly questionable whether anyone would decide to turn up to the wedding of their king dressed as the 'skeleton figure of death', as is implied. It would, therefore, seem that this suggestion was an attempt to explain away the version of the story stating it had been a skeleton that had appeared at the wedding. In doing so, and stating it was an act of 'jest', or a joke, however, this contradicts earlier versions of the story where there is no evidence that the figure was ever identified.

The second ghost connected to this area is the spirit of a woman who has been seen wandering around the site of the monument. She is normally referred to as the grey lady due to her shadow-like appearance, but some reports state that she is seen wearing a green dress.

Apparently she is also seen walking along the road and there have been many accounts of motorists swerving to avoid a woman, only to turn around and discover there was no one there. There has been speculation that this lady is the ghost of Yolande de Dreux, still mourning the loss of her husband. On the other hand, the ghost has also been seen in the Kingswood Hotel, which stands very close to the monument, and cannot, therefore, be Yolande de Dreux since the hotel building was not constructed until many centuries after her death.

Due to there being a general absence of documented reports of the ghost, I contacted the owners of the hotel directly and they were kind enough to provide some additional information from their own experiences. They advised that, despite having operated the hotel for almost three decades, they have never actually witnessed the ghost themselves. A few years ago, one of their regular guests did, however, have an encounter with her when he passed her in the upstairs corridor of the hotel. As she approached him he presumed she was just another guest but, as they passed each other, her presence caused a change in the atmosphere which made him shudder. He turned to try and see what had caused this feeling and found that the lady had vanished and the corridor was completely empty. Apparently the guest has never returned to the hotel!

They were also able to provide information that adds to my belief that the ghost is not that of Yolande de Dreux. They advised that, in the 1950s, she was often seen standing at the bus stop outside the hotel and the drivers of the buses would see her and stop to let her on, but by the time they had brought the bus to a

The Kingswood Hotel.

stop, no one was there. On one occasion, the woman did, however, step onto the bus and walk past the driver before climbing the stairs to the upper deck. This was at the time when conductors travelled on buses and so, once the woman had finished climbing the stairs, the conductress signalled to the driver to continue their journey and she went upstairs to collect the passenger's fare. As the reader may expect by now, she found the top deck of the bus empty. The conductress alerted the driver, who stopped the bus and they both searched for the lady but there was no one on board.

This story has been covered by the online magazine *The Kirkcaldy Book*, which goes further to say that the route became so unpopular with drivers after this incident that it was cancelled. Unfortunately, the bus company that operated in this area at the time has not

done so for a long time and so it has not been possible to obtain any further details from the staff at the bus garage.

If the ghost is not that of Yolande, the question of who she is remains unanswered. Local legend has it that she is the spirit of a woman who lived in a cottage behind the hotel building who hanged herself. *The Kirkcaldy Book* provides a story in which it reports that, while the property was still a private home, prior to being converted into a hotel, a young girl named Patsy Jean Fagan lived at the house with her parents, grandmother and uncle. The family knew of the ghost and named her Jenny, but it seemed that initially Jenny took a particular dislike to Patsy, frequently chasing her and nipping her 'like a goose', especially it seems when she wore a particular pair of red trousers that her mother had made her.

Jenny soon seems to have warmed to Patsy, however, and, on one occasion, Patsy had decided to explore the land to the rear of the hotel and climbed the steep, rocky hillside. Once she reached the top, she eventually turned to look back and realised how high she had climbed. Knowing she would not be able to get back down and fearful for her own safety, she climbed behind a rock and began to weep. A short while later, she felt as though someone was with her and she looked over to see a beautiful lady dressed in a long white dress. Patsy was immediately filled with a feeling of warmth and all her fears subsided as she looked at the woman. Her attention was suddenly drawn to voices and, when she looked, she saw her father had climbed up to her rescue. She turned to once again look at the lady in white whose presence alone had been enough to calm her, but she had vanished.

It is fair to assume that the ghost named Jenny is the woman still seen in the Kingswood Hotel, as the spirit appears to know her way around the building, and it is likely this is the same woman who is seen outside the hotel and at the bus stop. Unfortunately, until such time as more information becomes available, it seems likely that her true identity will remain a mystery.

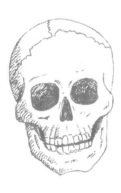

9

PISTOLS AT DAWN

A matter of honour led to one of the last pistol duels to take place in Scotland, and the haunting of Balmuto Castle, which sits approximately 3 miles west of Kirkcaldy.

Balmuto Castle was built in the early fifteenth century on behalf of Sir John Boswell, initially as a defensive three-storey tower house, with 2m-thick stone walls and an entrance on the first floor. Over the coming centuries, the castle was extensively extended and remodelled to create more comfortable living accommodation and it remained in the Boswell family until 1951 when, with no direct heirs, it was sold as a roofless ruin. Some nine years later, ownership of the castle returned to the Boswell family when Harry Boswell, a respected American lawyer and descendent of Sir John Boswell, bought the castle and restored it to its former glory.

The incident that led to the haunting of the castle took place in March 1822, involving Sir Alexander Boswell of Balmuto and a local man named James Stuart. Alexander Boswell was born in

October 1775 and grew to be described as a tall and muscular man. He had initially been destined for a career in law, but after the death of his father when he was just 19 years old, he found himself with a considerable inheritance in land and money and he soon ended his studies to concentrate on improving the agriculture on his lands. He held a commanding officer role in the Ayrshire Yeomanry, an independent cavalry troop, and also pursued a career as a poet and a politician. In the Oxford Dictionary of National Biography he is described as a 'thoroughgoing Tory', who had a particular dislike for the Whigs, a political party who were the main rivals to the Tories from the 1680s and that later evolved into the Liberal Party. Boswell is said to have considered the Whigs to be 'dangerous maniacs'.

Boswell became increasingly disillusioned with politics, feeling that he did not receive the respect or recognition that he deserved and, in 1821, due to a mixture of frustration and financial problems, he resigned from the House

Balmuto Castle.

of Commons. This, however, was not the end of his political life and he turned his attention towards James Stuart of Dunearn, a writer and a Whig politician.

In 1822, a number of articles were published by a Glasgow-based newspaper which was known to support the Tory party, *The Glasgow Sentinel*. These articles criticised the Whigs and seemed to singularly pick out James Stuart for ridicule. One article, published anonymously and entitled the 'Whig Song', implied Stuart was both a coward and a bully, leading Stuart to take action against the publishers of the paper for libel. A dispute between the publishers delayed the proceedings, during which time the original manuscripts for the offensive articles were, possibly illegally, made available to Stuart. While reading them, he recognised the handwriting to be that of Alexander Boswell, who he knew personally. The reason why Stuart had become the target of Boswell's attacks remains unclear; although they both represented opposing political parties and would have had very different opinions, there had not previously been any sign of conflict between the two men. At the time that the manuscripts were passed on to Stuart, Boswell was in London attending his brother's funeral. Upon his return to his home in Edinburgh, he was met with the Earl of Rosslyn, who had a note from Stuart detailing his grievance and asking that Boswell confirmed whether or not he was the author of the offensive material. Boswell refused to admit that

he had written them, but also refused to deny it, saying that Stuart had all the information he needed. Feeling unsatisfied with the outcome and still seeking retribution for the slur on his character, Stuart challenged him to a duel.

The traditional duel was quite different from how they are shown in popular movies. There were strict rules that applied and the arrangements were quite dignified, which may seem strange given the potentially fatal consequences. Both parties were required to appoint a 'second', a trusted person who would act on their behalf at the duel to ensure that everything was set up and carried out fairly. The seconds would agree the location of the duel, sometimes referred to as 'the field of honour', the time of the duel and the distance apart that the two parties would stand. It was up to the offended party to decide when the dual would be over. It was normal for each to fire a single shot, with the challenger either opting to shoot first, or electing that both parties were to shoot at the same time. In the event that neither were hit, the challenger could at that point deem that they were satisfied and, as the conditions of the duel had been fulfilled, the duel would be declared as over without either party losing their honour. This created an opportunity for both to deliberately miss to conclude the dispute, although this was forbidden in the rules. Alternatively the challenger could decide that the shots would continue to be exchanged until one party was either wounded or killed, although it was generally deemed that no more than three rounds of shots should be taken.

The duel between Sir Alexander Boswell and James Stuart was initially to take place in Edinburgh, but the local sheriff, when he became aware of the dispute, had both men arrested and only released them on condition that they kept the peace within the county and city of Edinburgh. The duel therefore took place in Fife in a field just outside Kirkcaldy on the morning of Tuesday, 26 March 1822. The distance was set at 12 paces, which was measured and agreed by the seconds. The identical pistols were then loaded with equal amounts of gunpowder to ensure that neither party had an advantage. It had been agreed both would shoot at the same time and, after they assumed their positions and had taken aim, the command was given and they both fired.

Boswell's shot missed, but he was not so lucky as Stuart's shot hit him in the shoulder, with the ball breaking his collarbone and travelling down to his spine. The outcome seemed surprising, given that Boswell was an accomplished military man, whereas Stuart had never fired a gun before in his life. Boswell was immediately taken to nearby Balmuto Castle, the home of his relative, where two surgeons from Kirkcaldy attended to him but unfortunately he died the following day.

James Stuart was charged with murder and a much-publicised trial followed. In the papers published after the trial, it was revealed that, as they prepared for the duel, Sir Alexander Boswell had stated to his second that he bore no ill will against Stuart and intended to fire into the air to deliberately miss. After he had been shot, he explained he had feared that he might not have raised his pistol high enough to show his intent to Stuart. In his defence, Stuart confirmed he had no inclination that it had been Boswell's intention to deliberately miss and, had he known, he would have been satisfied and would not have gone ahead with the duel. On 11 June 1822, after a trial that lasted just one day with the jury considering the evidence overnight, Stuart was found not guilty.

According to local legend, the ghost of Sir Alexander Boswell has been seen inside Balmuto Castle. Exact details of the sightings are unfortunately somewhat lacking, possibly due to the castle being abandoned in 1896, just seventy-four years after the incident, meaning there was no one there to witness any apparition until it was once again occupied after being restored. From the information available, it would seem the ghost has been seen on the main staircase of the tower and also in the library. The connection with the library may be due to the popular belief that the library door was taken from the castle and used as a makeshift stretcher to carry the injured Sir Boswell from the duel site back to the castle. There is, however, no mention of this in the records of James Stuart's trial, and it is instead suggested that Boswell was in fact carried to the castle on a horse.

Despite the lack of documented sightings to support the reports that the castle is haunted, consideration must be given to the circumstances surrounding Alexander Boswell's death. From the court papers, it seems clear he never intended to cause any real upset to James Stuart and it was only through his refusal to admit to penning the articles that he found himself in a situation where he not only faced taking the life of someone he bore no grudge against, but also put his own life in peril. Despite duelling pistols being notoriously inaccurate, he must have still known that his military experience gave him a considerable advantage over Stuart, hence taking the decision to deliberately fire into the air. It would seem he regretted the situation he had found himself in, a situation that would ultimately lead to his prolonged, painful death. The facts of this unfortunate incident provide the classic ingredients for a ghost story.

Please note Balmuto Castle is a private home and the privacy of the owners should be respected. The castle can be viewed from the edge of the village of Auchtertool or from Auchertool Kirk.

10

FURTHER AFIELD

ALTHOUGH this book concentrates on locations in Kirkcaldy and the surrounding area, journeying just a few miles further out there are several other locations well worth a mention.

Aberdour Castle

The coastal village of Aberdour is approximately 8 miles south of Kirkcaldy centre. It is here, beside the railway station, that you will find possibly the oldest standing stone-built castle in Scotland.

The large, partially ruinous, fortified house started life, like many Scottish castles, as a tower house and, dating back to the twelfth century, the remains of this tower are the oldest part of the castle as it stands today. Originally owned by the Mortimer family, it was not until the estate was passed to the Douglas family in 1351 that the castle began to grow. During the fifteenth century, the tower house was heightened and over the centuries that followed, the castle was successively remodelled and extended to

change from the original defensive structure, to an extensive, luxurious home.

Unfortunately, the castle was extensively damaged by a fire in the seventeenth century and, despite plans being prepared for the restoration and a further extension to the castle, the family moved to the neighbouring Aberdour House. Following another fire in the eighteenth century, the majority of the castle was left uninhabitable (with the exception of the east range, the only part of the building that had remained roofed) and it remained abandoned for two centuries, during which time there was extensive deterioration in the structure and the central range and tower began to collapse. The east range continued to be used, but only as an army barrack, a schoolroom and a hall – it was never to be used as a home again. In 1924, the castle was placed under the guardianship of the HM Office of Works, a department initially responsible for overseeing the building of castles and residences for the Royal Family, which by the twentieth century was responsible

East range, Aberdour Castle.

Another view of Aberdour Castle.

for looking after public buildings. Work to restore the gardens and stabilise the castle ruins was carried out over the following decades. The castle is now looked after and operated by Historic Scotland.

Aberdour Castle is said to have been haunted by a grey lady for a very long time, yet there appears to be little information available about who she may be. The ghost, who only appears within the castle grounds, does not seem to interact with her witnesses and is said to be a haunting of a benign nature. However, an incident is said to have taken place some years ago when a group of craftsmen arrived to carry out some work on the castle. Finding it to be locked, they sought shelter from the wind in the cover of the stable door and, as they waited for the key holder to arrive, they heard heavy furniture being dragged across the floor above them. Concerned by the noises, as they were aware the castle should be empty, they watched the locked door for anyone coming out. The key holder arrived a short while later and, after telling her what they had heard, they entered the castle. In one room, they found several items of furniture in the middle. This was said to be replica medieval furniture, most of which required two people to lift. Despite a search, no one was found to have been in the castle, and all of the doors and windows remained locked, yet had anyone been inside and left via the main door, they would have been spotted by the craftsmen. Like the grey lady, the identity of whoever is responsible for moving the furniture remains a mystery. It does seem this is a not too uncommon occurrence, with the sounds of furniture being moved heard by several people, although the incident with the craftsmen seems to have been the only instance when the furniture was actually found out of place.

Rossend Castle

Rossend Castle sits in a dominant position on a cliff top overlooking the coastal town of Burntisland, a few miles south of Kirkcaldy. Over the years, the impressive-looking, four-storey, T-shaped tower house has undergone considerable alterations and extensions since its early origins.

A castle is known to have stood on the site since 1119, although at that time it comprised solely of a traditional stone keep, known as the Tower of Kinghorne Wester (to avoid confusion with Glamis Castle in Angus – the childhood home of Queen Elizabeth, the Queen Mother – which was then known as the Tower of Kinghorne Easter). The tower was also known as Burntisland Castle. At some point the original keep tower was extended and, although exact details or the dates of this work are not known, the records held by Historic Scotland show that by 1382 the property was known as Abbot's Hall and was in the ownership of the Abbots of Dunfermline (who, the reader may recall from the introduction to this book, were responsible for the initial development of the town of Kirkcaldy). It is therefore reasonable to assume the alterations were carried out prior to it becoming home to the abbot, who is likely to have required a more comfortable home than the basic keep tower. In 1538, George Durie, the then Abbot of Dunfermline, gifted the castle to his son, Peter, and in 1552 he started extensive remodelling and extension work. This work, which was not completed until 1554, included rebuilding the original keep tower, incorporating parts of the 1119 original structure on the ground floor.

Rossend Castle, side view.

In 1560, during the Scottish Reformation, the castle was taken from the Duries and given to the Melville family, prior to being passed to Sir William Kirkcaldy of Grange who owned it until his execution in 1573. In 1581, King James VI returned the castle to the ownership of the Melville family, who carried out further alterations and extensions to the building, which included an ornate painted ceiling that is believed to have been completed in anticipation of the king's visit to the castle in 1617. In the mid-seventeenth century, the Covenanters occupied the castle during the Scottish Civil War until it was taken by Oliver Cromwell's forces and returned to the Melville family.

The castle continued to pass between prominent families of the time, including Murdoch Campbell, a writer and merchant from the Isle of Skye, who is believed to have been responsible for renaming the castle Rossend, an old Celtic name. Each of these families carried out their own extensions and alterations to the castle and it continued to grow in stature from the original tower. In 1873, James Shepherd, owner of one of Kirkcaldy's linoleum factories, purchased the castle and stayed there until his death in 1907, when the castle was bought by Burntisland Town Council. The council were, however, not so much interested in the castle itself, but more concerned with the land that came with it. They required the rights to the land in front of the castle to extend the docks, which they acquired through the purchase of the castle, and they used the surrounding land and parts of the other buildings on the site to create housing.

With no real use for the castle, other than a brief spell as a boarding school, the building was left empty and began to deteriorate. Fortunately, the painted ceiling dating from 1617, which had been covered up during later remodelling, was rediscovered in 1952 and moved to the National Museum of Scotland in Edinburgh as, by the 1960s, the building was in such a poor state that proposals were made to demolish it. Had the painted ceiling not been removed, it almost certainly would have been lost.

The intention to demolish the castle faced fierce local opposition and, in 1972, the decision was made that it should not be demolished and was to be saved. In 1975 – by which time it was a roofless ruin – the castle was purchased by a firm of architects, who spent two years restoring the castle to its former glory to be used as their offices. During the restoration, two secret staircases were discovered, along with the ground-floor vaults. The castle was recently put up for sale and, although it was removed from the market, there are no records of the sale being concluded and it appears to once again stand empty.

There have been several references in publications throughout the years to Rossend Castle being haunted yet, other than saying 'by a ghost' (which would seem obvious!), there is very little other information as to what was actually experienced in the castle. I was, however, lucky enough to gain some additional information from an acquaintance who used to work at the castle. The spiral staircase, as you enter the castle, goes down a few steps to the ground floor, or up to the first floor, and was described as feeling particularly 'eerie', with another person who used to frequent the castle also telling me that he would always run up the stairs when visiting after dark.

Rossend Castle, front view.

In the main body of the castle, on the first, second and third floor, are areas known as the great halls, each measuring around 16m by 6m. These large, open spaces were used as the main office areas, with a reception and private offices being formed in the side wings. It was from these side offices that reports were made of footsteps being heard either coming from the great halls or on the staircase when, aside from the person witnessing the noises, the building was empty. Shadows of figures have also reportedly been glimpsed momentarily, although in fact there was no one there.

The lack of formal documentation leaves the question of who might be responsible for these strange occurrences and feelings of unease within the castle. The answer may lie with an incident that took place in 1563 when Mary, Queen of Scots, stayed overnight at the castle while travelling to St Andrews. The queen is

known to have stayed at the castle on a number of occasions and one of the rooms is still known as Queen Mary's room. On this occasion, however, she was to have a particularly unpleasant visit. Having retired for the night, a man was discovered hiding in the room. The cries for help from the queen and her ladies in waiting soon brought the assistance of others in the castle and the man was captured. He was found to be Pierre du Chastelard, a young French nobleman who had been attached to the household of Marshall Damville.

Details of the incident are documented in the book *Mary Stuart* by Alexandre Dumas, published in 1910. This tells that Mary had previously stayed with the Damville household during a visit to France, and Chastelard had assisted in attending to the queen during this time. However, Chastelard, who was also a poet, became besotted with Mary and began to write poems for her. The queen was pleased to receive these poems, and it seems Chastelard took her enjoyment in his words as a sign that she too had feelings for him, which only served to encourage him further. When Mary returned to Scotland, unaware of his growing obsession, Chastelard was sent with her to tend to her needs during the journey, during which time he became convinced that there was a mutual attraction between them. His passion for the queen was to lead him to take extreme action and, on one evening, as Mary prepared for bed at Holyrood Palace in Edinburgh, her dog began to bark at something under the bed. The room was checked and it was discovered Chastelard was hiding there.

On this occasion, which had taken place about three weeks before the incident in Rossend Castle, Mary had forgiven Chastelard, and this act of kindness was to further convince him that the love he felt for the queen was reciprocated. His belief led him to then follow her to Burntisland where he repeated his attempt to get her alone in her bedchamber, and this time he almost succeeded, only being found in a cupboard after the queen was already in bed.

On this instance, however, Mary was not so forgiving and it is said she had initially demanded that he be killed on the spot. It was instead decided that he should stand trial and so he was held and taken to St Andrews, where he was charged and found guilty. A week later, in front of a large crowd and with the queen watching, he was beheaded. It is reported that, just before his execution, he looked towards the queen and shouted 'Adieu, loveliest and most cruel of princesses', and so it would seem he took his love for the queen to the grave with him.

Given the extent of his actions, it could be considered that Chastelard's feelings went beyond an obsession and most would deem it to have been insanity that would lead him to believe that he could repeat his attempts to hide in the queen's bedchamber without any consequences. With an apparently unstable character connected with the castle, the last place he saw the queen before his execution, it is possible that the fleeting glimpses of a figure seemingly keen to stay out of sight and the footsteps of someone moving around the castle while all else is quiet are manifestations of the spirit of Pierre du Chastelard, still seeking the love of his life, Mary, Queen of Scots.

Balgonie Castle

Close to the village of Milton of Balgonie, approximately 6 miles north of Kirkcaldy, sits Balgonie Castle. The tower house of the castle is historically significant as, dating back to the late fourteenth century, it it is the oldest complete surviving tower house in the Kingdom of Fife.

The castle was originally built for Sir Thomas Sibbald of Balgonie (no connection to Mary Sibbald of the Wemyss caves), prior to it being passed, through marriage, to the Lord High Treasurer of Scotland, Sir Robert Lundie, in the fifteenth century. Sir Lundie carried out the initial extensions to the original tower house by adding a new wing to the north east, which incorporated an existing chapel and courtyard tower, to provide larger, more comfortable living accommodation. Oddly, he left a gap between the tower and the wing, effectively meaning they were two separate buildings. It is thought the gap was left for the purpose of defence, although it is difficult to see how this achieved the goal of making the building more homely.

Throughout the centuries, the castle passed through the ownership of several notable families, each of whom carried out their own alterations and extensions, one of which included building a stair tower in the gap between the earlier wing and tower to create a single building. The castle also welcomed many well-known figures, including King James IV, Dr Benjamin Rush and Mary, Queen of Scots and, for a short time, was held by Rob Roy MacGregor. Unfortunately, by the mid-nineteenth century the castle was no longer being used as a home and it started to fall

Balgonie Castle.

into a state of disrepair. The roof was later removed to avoid paying tax for the building, which resulted in a rapid increase of the rate of decay and it quickly became a ruin.

In 1971, the remains of the castle were purchased by a private owner and a restoration project commenced, concentrating on the original tower house. The present owners purchased it in 1985, and they have continued with the sympathetic restoration. Although this is still ongoing, much of the castle has already been saved, with the original features being retained. As well as having the castle as a family home, the owners offer the opportunity for people to hold their weddings there. The chapel in the northeast wing has been restored, as has the great hall, and between them they provide the facilities for both the wedding ceremony and a banquet after.

Although Balgonie is again an impressive-looking castle, often filled with the happiness of a wedding, the castle has a long history of reports of hauntings and certainly seems to have more than its fair share of phantoms. One of these is described as a green lady, meaning a female spirit that normally appears either green in appearance or is wearing a green dress. Green lady spirits are common in Scotland and are generally considered to mean no harm to those who see them, with some considering them to be protectors of those who occupy the buildings. Believed to be a member of the Lundie family, she is frequently referred to as Green Jeanie, although she is not the same 'Green Jean' of Wemyss Castle, and recordings of her being witnessed date back to 1842, where she is referred to as 'a well-known phantom'.

Green Jeanie is not the only ghost to be seen in the castle. Witnesses have also encountered a soldier, dressed in what appears to be seventeenth-century clothing, walking around the courtyard area and sometimes out through the gates of the castle. Less well-documented spectres include that of a hooded figure who is possibly a religious character, an elderly looking man and even a disembodied head that floats around the corridors. Unfortunately, there is little information as to who these are, although another ghost has been identified following several reports of sightings of a tall man being seen walking within the castle. Witnesses saw him so clearly that they were later able to identify him as the first Earl of Leven, Alexander Leslie (who died in the castle in 1661), from his portrait that still hangs in the castle. If the human spirits were not enough,

the castle also lays claim to a ghostly dog that has been spotted running around the grounds.

In addition to the actual sightings of figures, there are also claims of unexplained sounds from within the castle, which seem to be concentrated on the great hall. People attending functions at the castle have reported hearing conversations taking place around them in whispered voices, which they are certain are not coming from any of the other guests. Perhaps the many ghosts of the castle also enjoy coming along to the festivities after a wedding at the castle.

There is no doubt that Balgonie Castle is an interesting building and why there is so much paranormal activity reported has not yet been explained. With ongoing restoration work, perhaps further secrets held by the castle will be revealed in the future.

A NOTE ON THE TEXT

I hope you have enjoyed this collection of stories from Kirkcaldy and the surrounding area. As mentioned in the introduction, the biggest challenge in compiling this book was sourcing the information. In the past, the initial stages of my research have involved surrounding myself with countless books covering the local history, folklore and 'ghost stories' for a number of weeks to select suitable locations for further investigation. It quickly became apparent, however, that there was a distinct lack of reports of ghostly goings-on in Kirkcaldy and that a wider exploration would be required. While this involved far more extensive research and piecing together segments of information to bring together the stories, it was also quite satisfying to know that this book may well be the first time these stories have been brought together into one binding.

Although I consider myself to be relatively knowledgeable on haunted locations, particularly in the County of Fife, my research for this book revealed that there is a lot I didn't know! Certainly I had not heard the many tales relating to Michael Scott, the Wizard of the North, and, although I only mention him in passing here, there is so much more this great man is said to have done that one of my next projects will be researching these in greater detail. I am also keen to find out more about the quarrying of stone from Bel Crag and plan to carry out research in this area. Reference is made to many stately homes around the country containing stone from this area, and it will be interesting to find out whether any of these homes have ghost stories associated with them that could be traced back to Bel Crag. It is also interesting to note that Kirkcaldy seems to have more than its fair share of reports coming from private homes, which raises the possibility that these too may have been at least partially constructed from the smaller stones from Bel Crag and could still carry some of the energy said to have been emitted from the area.

One thing that did cross my mind as I was writing the book was the lack of reported haunted locations within the town of Kirkcaldy itself. There are smaller towns nearby that seem to have far more ghosts: St Andrews for example. I, however, believe this has to do with the way Kirkcaldy grew and its lack of involvement in any significant conflicts. The original town stayed along the coast and it was only in the 1900s that significant growth started. There is, however, another possible reason, which is revealed in one of the few incidents covered by the press. On 5 February 1875, the *Northern Warder and Bi-Weekly Courier* carried a story titled 'A Kirkcaldy Ghost Story'. The article reported that for several days there had been sightings of a figure in white appearing close to one of the town's factories, terrifying the local women who worked there to such an extent that they refused to walk alone to and from work and now did so only in groups. It goes on to tell how a man had also witnessed the figure as he walked along Mid Street on his way home. The description given was that the ghost 'appeared to be about eight feet tall, clothed in white, with a very ugly visage, and that he disappeared as suddenly as he came, appearing to be springing rather than walking'. While reports such as this in towns and cities throughout the country would have lead to hysteria and the paranormal experts of the time or the local priest being called upon to try to resolve the matter, the hard-working people of old industrial Kirkcaldy had a different way of dealing with it. The paper goes on to report that 'for several nights a number of young men have been scouring the neighbourhood, armed with large sticks, in search of the ghost'. No further mention is made of the incidents and the actions taken indicate a clear unwillingness of the locals at the time to consider them to have anything other than a natural explanation, with the instant conclusion being that it was a prankster who deserved to be taught a lesson. With opinions such as these, it is very likely that many unexplained incidents were simply dismissed as someone playing a joke and never reported or recorded, resulting in the lack of historical data covering the potentially haunted locations.

With that said, in January 2014 the press reported a court case in which a 61-year-old woman was charged with attacking her older sister. It was reported that the woman claimed that her house in Kirkcaldy was haunted by several spirits, with experiences such as her dog transforming into a beast (referred to as a hell hound) and growling at her. The dog's water bowl was also said to move around the property with no apparent physical cause and the woman claimed that she could not sleep due to the spirits within the property. Her older sister, on one particular visit, expressed concern for her sister's health and suggested seeking medical advice. The atmosphere seems to have been calm while the sisters discussed the situation, yet, when a friend arrived, the younger sister's mood is said to have completely changed and she became aggressive, demanding that they leave and attacking her older sister, knocking her unconscious. It may well be that the town of Kirkcaldy has not yet revealed all of its ghosts.

I would like to take the opportunity to remind readers that some of the locations mentioned, such as Balmuto Tower and Wemyss Castle are private residences that are not open to the public and the owner's privacy should be respected.

I always welcome feedback and am interested to hear about other people's experiences. I can be contacted at my website: http://gstewartauthor.com.

BIBLIOGRAPHY

Books and Publications

Anon., *Castles & Heritage Trail of Fife: Ravenscraig Castle Trail* (West Wemyss Environmental Education Centre, Undated)

Anon., *Trial of James Stuart for the murder of Sir Alexander Boswell* (Edinburgh: J. Dick and Co., 1822)

Bonthrone, Eila, *Fife and its Folk; A Key to the 'Kingdom'* (Edinburgh: C.J. Cousland & Sons, 1951)

Boucher, Robert, *The Kingdom of Fife: Its Ballads and Legends* (Dundee: John Leng & Co., 1899)

Bowler, Walter, *Scotichronicon Book VI*, ed. and trans. D.E.R. Watt (Aberdeen and Edinburgh: Aberdeen University Press/ Mercat Press, 1995)

Chalmers, Robert, *Domestic Annals of Scotland: From the Reformation to the Revolution* (Edinburgh: W. & R. Chalmers, 1874)

Chambers, R. and W. Chambers, *Gazeteers of Scotland, 1803–1901* (National Library of Scotland, online edn, 2012 http://digital.nls.uk/gazetteers-of-scotland-1803-1901/pageturner.cfm?id=97430894&mode=transcription, accessed 5 October 2013)

Chalmers, Robert, *Popular Rhymes, Fireside Stories and Amusements of Scotland* (Edinburgh: William and Robert Chalmers, 1842)

Coventry, Martin, *Scottish Ghosts and Bogles* (Musselburgh: Goblinshead, 2004)

Crowe, Catherine, *The Night Side of Nature: or Ghosts and Ghost Seers* (London: George Routledge & Sons, 1904)

Dalrymple, David, *Annales of Scotland* (London: J. Murray, 1776)

Dumas, Alexandre, *Mary Stuart* (P.F. Collier, 1910)

Evans, M.S., *Castles and Churches in Fife* (Glenrothes: The Dolphin Press, 1998)

Fawcett, Richard, *Castles of Fife; A Heritage Guide* (Fife Regional Council, 1993)

Fisher, D.R., *Boswell, Sir Alexander, first baronet (1775–1822)* (Oxford Dictionary of National Biography, Oxford

University Press, 2004; online edn,
May 2005 www.oxforddnb.com/view/
article/2947, accessed 11 November 2013)

Fraser, Duncan, *Historic Fife* (Perth: Melven
Press, 1982)

Geddie, John, *The Fringes of Fife* (Edinburgh
and London: W. & R. Chalmers, New and
Enlarged Edition, 1927)

Gilchrist, A., *Lambkin: A Study in Evolution*
(English Folk Dance & Song Society, 1932)

Groome, Francis, *Ordnance Gazetteer of
Scotland: A Survey of Scottish Topography*
(Edinburgh: Thomas C. Jack, 1884)

Lang, Theo, *The King's Scotland;
The Kingdom of Fife* (London: Hodder
and Stoughton, 1951)

Leighton, Alexander, *Wilson's Tales of the
Borders and of Scotland* Vols VII & VIII
(Glasgow: John McGready, Undated)

Leighton, John M., *History of the County of
Fife* (Glasgow: Joseph Swan, 1811)

Lindsay, Robert, *The History of Scotland:
From 21st February 1436 to March 1565*
(Edinburgh: Baskett and Company, 1728)

McKay, Charles, *The Legendary and
Romantic Ballads of Scotland* (London:
Griffin Bohn & Co., 1861)

Millar, A.H., *Fife: Pictorial and Historical* Vols
I & II (Cupar: A Westwood & Son, 1895)

Munster, The Countess of, *My Memories and
Miscellanies* (London: Eveleigh Nash, 1904)

Pease, Howard, *Border Ghost Stories*
(London: Erskine MacDonald Ltd, 1919)

Scales, J.K., *Of Kindred Celtic Origins*
(Lincoln: iUniverse, 2001)

Scott, Walter, *The Poetical Works of Sir Walter
Scott* (Edinburgh: Robert Caldwell, 1841)

Simpkins, John Ewart, *County Folk-Lore Vol.
VII Examples of Printed Folk-Lore Concerning
Fife with some notes on Clackmannan and
Kinross-shires* (London: The Folklore
Society/Sidgwick & Jackson, 1914)

Westwood, J. and S. Kingshill, *The Lore of
Scotland* (Random House Books, 2009)

Underwood, Peter, *Gazetteer of Scottish
& Irish Ghosts* (London: Souvenir
Press, 1975)

Various, *Descriptive Account of the Principle
Towns in Scotland* (Edinburgh, 1828)

Various, *Raising the Bar* (Edinburgh:
Historic Scotland, 2009)

Various, *The Kingdom of Fife in Days Gone By*
(Lang Syne Publishers Ltd, Undated)

Magazines

Duke of Argyll, 'Real Ghost
Stories', in *The London Magazine*,
November 1901

Harrower-Gray, A., 'A Towering Tale'
in *Scotland Magazine*, Issue 49,
February 2010

Harrower-Gray, A., 'The Haunting of
Wemyss' in *Scotland Magazine*, Issue 52,
August 2010

Newspapers

Fife Free Press, 24 February 2005,
28 October 2010

The Northern Warder and Bi-Weekly Courier,
5 February 1875

The Scotsman, 23 April 2006

The Weekly Scotsman, 26 December 1896

Websites

Auchtertool Parish Kirk:
http://auchtertoolkirk.org.uk

Balgonie Castle: www.balgoniecastle.co.uk

BBC Doomsday Reloaded:
www.bbc.co.uk/history/domesday/
dblock/GB-332000-696000/page/17

Dictionary of Scottish Architects 1840–1980:
www.scottisharchitects.org.uk/building_
full.php?id=203985

Ghost Finders Scotland:
www.ghostfinders.co.uk

Haunted Scotland:
  http://haunted-scotland.co.uk
Historic Scotland:
  www.historic-scotland.gov.uk
Kirkcaldy Old Kirk Trust:
  www.kirkcaldyoldkirktrust.org.uk
National Library of Scotland: www.nls.uk

Royal Commission on the Ancient and
  Historical Monuments of Scotland:
  www.rcahms.gov.uk
Society for Psychical Research:
  www.spr.ac.uk
The Kirkcaldy Book:
  www.kirkcaldybook.com

Also from The History Press

More spooky Books

Lightning Source UK Ltd.
Milton Keynes UK
UKOW04f1318120814

236816UK00001B/1/P